Del has done a fabulous job in collecting stories, testimonies, and nuggets from many major league players and coaches in their walk with our Lord. *Dugout Devotions II* is inspirational and transforming for all ages. I am blessed to be included in this book and love walking side by side with Del in providing honest examples of Christian mentorship.

—Dave Jauss, bench coach, New York Yankees

Dugout Devotions II is another inspirational hit that is sure to strengthen your walk with the Lord. Author Del Duduit once again combines the love of baseball with Christian principles in a way that will encourage anyone who reads this book. Inside the pages, you will read about the faith of some of the biggest names in professional baseball and what Jesus Christ means to them. I am once again humbled to be a part of the second *Dugout Devotions* and locking arms and running errands for Jesus with my friend Del.

—Clint Hurdle, retired MLB manager and player

My friend and author Del Duduit has written an encouraging sequel to *Dugout Devotions*. I was honored to be included in the first one, but I am just as excited to read *Dugout Devotions II*. This game of life is not easy, and we all need inspiration and motivation to keep swinging, even when we are down for the count. This book has those components. I like how Del took his personal interviews with some MLB stars and turned t´ all need every day. This is a grand s

—1

I love Jesus with all my heart and as a former professional baseball player, I have a passion for the game of baseball. I truly appreciate how author Del Duduit has intertwined the two topics (faith in Jesus and baseball) with both motivational and inspirational messages from well-known players and coaches in Major League Baseball. These testimonies of faith from players are weaved with messages of hope as well as salvation for everyone to read and receive. This book, *Dugout Devotions II*, will be a blessing to you and your walk with Jesus Christ.

—Stan Lovins II, evangelist,
president of Sandlot Ministries

Throughout life, you will be pitched some difficult balls to hit. But if you work hard, practice, and stay close to God, you will never strike out. In *Dugout Devotions II*, you will read about how MLB All-Stars relied on their faith in the Lord to see them through challenging times. The best way to enjoy this life and hit a home run is to let God swing the bat for you. I am blessed to be a small part of *Dugout Devotions II*.

—Al Oliver, World Series champion,
National League batting champion

Wow . . . Del Duduit does it again in *Dugout Devotions II*. Whenever big-name athletes give big-time testimonies, it's a sure-fire recipe for success. With his insightful spiritual commentary and his passionate love for God, Del takes everything to a brand-new level. Another divine Grand Slam!

—Dr. John Huang, Nolan Media Group

Del Duduit is a master storyteller. You don't just read what Del writes but rather you become immersed in what is written as if you were there just beyond his shoulder listening to the conversation as it unfolded. You will enjoy *Dugout Devotions II*, and you will consider it time well spent again and again.

—Dave MacDonald, cohost of the
Exercise Your Faith podcast

Del Duduit has taken his reporter experience and given you another excellent book of devotions. *Dugout Devotions II* features players and coaches of great faith. The **"On Deck"** and "**Step Up to the Plate**" features in the book help you apply faith lessons to your life.

—Billie Jauss, author of *Making Room:
Doing Less So God Can Do More*

Other books in the Stars of the Faith Series

Dugout Devotions: Inspirational Hits from MLB's Best
First Down Devotions: Inspiration from NFL's Best
Auburn Believer: 40 Days of Devotions for the Tiger Faithful
Alabama Believer: 40 Days of Devotions for the Roll Tide Faithful

DUGOUT
DEVOTIONS II

MORE INSPIRATIONAL HITS FROM MLB'S BEST

DEL DUDUIT

IRON STREAM
B O O K S
An imprint of Iron Stream Media
Birmingham, Alabama

Iron Stream Books
100 Missionary Ridge
Birmingham, AL 35242
IronStreamMedia.com
Iron Stream Books is an imprint of Iron Stream Media

Library of Congress Control Number: 2021932079

ISBN-13: 978-1-56309-372-2
Ebook ISBN: 978-1-56309-373-9

Printed in the United State of America

1 2 3 4 5—25 24 23 22 21

This book is dedicated to my granddaughter, Sophie.

When you entered into our lives, you had an instant impact of fun.

I never had a sister growing up or a daughter to raise, so you were a new, fresh, and fun experience.

Your personality is addictive, and your smile is contagious.

Thank you for coming into our world and making it better and brighter.

I know you will be the best example of a kind and sweet person for your little brother to watch and learn from over the years. Take care of him please, and keep him out of trouble.

I remember watching you play T-ball and running the bases with enthusiasm and excitement every time you hit the ball. Do you remember the black-and-pink T-ball glove I gave you? You used it during your first season. I can't wait to watch you grow into a wonderful young lady, and I know you will always put God first in your life.

And I hope and pray at some point in your life, you will take time to sit down and be blessed and encouraged by the words in this little book that I wrote. I hope you treasure it as much as I treasure you.

Your grandmother and I love you with all our hearts.

Grandpa

CONTENTS

Acknowledgments   **xiii**

Foreword   **xv**
By Billie Jauss

Day 1: Shine the Best You Can for God   **1**
Tim Tebow: Outfielder, New York Mets
By Del Duduit

Day 2: God's Plan Works   **6**
José Altuve: All-Star and MVP Second Baseman,
   Houston Astros
By Del Duduit

Day 3: Work Hard with the Ability God Gives You   **11**
Francisco Lindor: All-Star Shortstop, Cleveland Indians
By Beckie Lindsey

Day 4: It's Not About Me   **16**
Michael Lorenzen: Pitcher, Cincinnati Reds
By Del Duduit

Day 5: Make It a Point to Inspire Hope   **22**
Clayton Kershaw: Multiple Cy Young Award–Winning Pitcher,
   Los Angeles Dodgers
By Clint Rutledge

Day 6: You Can Be Anything You Want   **27**
Albert Pujols: Multiple MVP Winner and First Baseman,
   Los Angeles Angels of Anaheim
By Del Duduit

Day 7: Impacting the Next Generation   **32**
Andrew McCutchen: Outfielder, New York Yankees and
     Former National League MVP
By Ryan Farr

Day 8: Put Aside the Ego   **37**
Brian Dozier: All-Star Second Baseman, Washington Nationals
By Del Duduit

Day 9: The Struggle with Sin   **42**
R. A. Dickey: Cy Young Award–Winning Pitcher,
     Atlanta Braves
By Cyle Young

Day 10: Praise Away the Devil's Attacks   **47**
Robinson Chirinos: Catcher, Houston Astros
By Del Duduit

Day 11: You Are One of a Kind to God   **52**
Adam Cimber: Pitcher, Cleveland Indians
By Del Duduit

Day 12: Understand God Loves You   **57**
Chris Davis: All-Star First Baseman, Baltimore Orioles
By Del Duduit

Day 13: First Big-League At-Bat Challenge   **63**
Tony Graffanino: Second Baseman, Atlanta Braves
By Scott McCausey

Day 14: God Will Take Care of You   **68**
Cody Allen: Pitcher, Los Angeles Angels of Anaheim
By Del Duduit

Day 15: Why Get Involved?   **73**
Tim Tebow: Outfielder, New York Mets
By Del Duduit

Day 16: Life Can Be a Walk in the Ballpark   **78**
Curtis Granderson: All-Star Outfielder, Miami Marlins
By Del Duduit

Day 17: Appreciate the Small Things   **83**
Daniel Norris: Pitcher, Detroit Tigers
By Del Duduit

Day 18: Do You Hear What He Says?   **88**
Dave Jauss: Coach and Scout, New York Yankees
By Del Duduit

Day 19: His Name Is Written Down   **93**
Al Oliver: Batting Champion, World Series Champion,
     Pittsburgh Pirates
By Del Duduit

Day 20: Why Are You Here?   **98**
Adam Cimber: Pitcher, Cleveland Indians
By Del Duduit

Day 21: Break the Slump   **103**
Chris Davis: All-Star First Baseman, Baltimore Orioles
By Del Duduit

Day 22: Let Your Voice Be Heard   **108**
Daniel Stumpf: Pitcher, Detroit Tigers
By Del Duduit

Day 23: What's Your Go-To Verse?   **113**
David Hess: Pitcher, Baltimore Orioles
By Del Duduit

Day 24: What Is Your Gift?   **118**
Al Oliver: Batting Champion, World Series Champion,
     Pittsburgh Pirates
By Del Duduit

Day 25: Make an Entrance   123
Corey Dickerson: All-Star Outfielder, Philadelphia Phillies
By Del Duduit

Day 26: Be Passionate in Your Service   127
Tim Tebow: Outfielder, New York Mets
By Del Duduit

Day 27: You Are Special to God   132
Clint Hurdle: MLB Player and Coach, Retired
By Del Duduit

Day 28: Start the Conversation   137
Curtis Granderson: All-Star Outfielder, Miami Marlins
By Del Duduit

Day 29: The Aha Moment   142
Spencer Turnbull: Pitcher, Detroit Tigers
By Del Duduit

Day 30: Grow with the Word   147
Jacob Stallings: Catcher, Pittsburgh Pirates
By Del Duduit

ACKNOWLEDGMENTS

The following people played a significant role in the completion of this book, and I want to thank them personally.

My wife, Angie, for being the initial editor and supporting me through this process.

My agent, Cyle Young, for his assistance in making this process a reality.

To Billie Jauss for writing the foreword and being a friend, as well as her husband, Dave.

To the Portsmouth Daily Times and their assistance with media credentials.

To the following for contributing a devotional in this book:

- Beckie Lindsey
- Clint Rutledge
- Ryan Farr
- Cyle Young
- Scott McCausey

To John Herring and Ramona Richards at Iron Stream Media and New Hope Publishers for their faith in me.

To Reagan Jackson and Susan Cornell for making this book better with their edits.

And to God for giving me this wonderful opportunity.

FOREWORD

I've learned a lot of lessons over our thirty-plus years in professional baseball. My husband has managed, coached, scouted, and worked in the front office over the years. Many years ago, my husband, David, and I learned to put Jesus at the center of our individual lives, our marriage, our family, and our work. These are the most valuable lessons of all.

Baseball became our mission field, each day working as if working for the Lord. David in the clubhouse, me in the stands. He has had many job titles but none more critical than a servant of Christ. Developing lives that have an eternal perspective is one of the incredible blessings of my life. Our relationship with others we work and sit alongside has strengthened our faith. It is an honor to glorify Jesus with these men and women.

Del Duduit has taken his reporter experience and given you another excellent book of devotions. *Dugout Devotions II* features players and coaches of great faith. The "On Deck" and "Step Up to the Plate" features in the book help you apply faith lessons to your life.

Not often do people outside the day-to-day operation of a baseball team get a glimpse of the incredible faith of the men inside the game. You will learn about their faith and how they walk it out in the professional baseball life.

I pray this book speaks to you, drawing you deeper into your relationship with Christ. There is no greater lesson than learning by the side of our Creator—more of Him, less of me.

Billie Jauss
Author of *Making Room: Doing Less So God Can Do More*

DAY 1
SHINE THE BEST YOU CAN FOR GOD

Tim Tebow:
Outfielder,
New York Mets

By Del Duduit

Why, even the hairs of your head are all numbered. Fear
not; you are of more value than many sparrows.

—Luke 12:7

When Tim Tebow first heard about a "Jesus Prom," he
thought it was a cool idea.

The Tim Tebow Foundation was about to reach its five-
year anniversary, and Tim wanted to do something special
for the occasion. The executive director of his foundation
knew about the "Jesus Prom," a night dedicated each year
to celebrate people with special needs.

Tim has a unique desire to help such people, and the
idea fit his mission.

"I loved it," Tim said. "I said I wanted to do the event
and have it everywhere—all over the country."

Tim spent many of his early years in the Philippines
where his parents served as missionaries. There he saw the
love his parents had for the people, and his parents instilled
the importance of serving others in his heart.

He said God's salvation gave him the responsibility to give back to others and make a difference in lives.

At the age of fifteen, he visited a remote village and met a boy who was born with his feet backward. Some thought of the boy as cursed, but Tim showed him the love of Christ by picking him up to hold him.

His passion to help others was born that day.

In 2010, his foundation was created.

Today, the Night to Shine is an evening dedicated to making thousands of people with special needs feel blessed.

"It's such a part of our identity and our worth about understanding how much God loves us," Tim said. "For us to be able to help this community to where the biggest event in their city and their town is for them to understand their worth. It's not enough that they know that we love them, but the God of this universe loves them."

The first year the Night to Shine was launched, it was held in forty-four cities.

In 2019, more than 655 churches participated and helped give more than 100,000 guests a Night to Shine provided by the hard work of more than 200,000 volunteers.

"After the first year, it just blew up, and it's so cool," Tim said. "It's such a blessing, and we are grateful to all the churches that help to have an impact on lives. It's my favorite night of the year, and I look forward to it so much. Right after it's over, we start planning for next year. We gather input from all over and make necessary adjustments on how we can improve."

For at least one night a year, guests can wear fancy dresses or tuxedos and attend a prom event where they are queen or king for the evening. They have their hair done just right and even have their shoes shined. A dinner is held in their honor, and their entrance into the ball room is announced to everyone in attendance.

> Because you are precious in my eyes,
> and honored, and I love you,
> I give men in return for you,
> peoples in exchange for your life.
>
> —Isaiah 43:4

Do you make the God of this universe feel special? Would He smile if you gave Him your attention?

On Deck

How would your spouse or best friend feel if you never paid them any attention? If you only stopped by to visit them two or three times a year, would they feel important? Probably not.

Step Up to the Plate

If you have not made the Lord feel special, you can start today. It's not as complicated as you might think. In fact, it's quite simple. Here are some steps you can take each day to make sure God knows where He stands in your life. Make His name shine.

1. Spend time with God. Set aside a few moments each morning or at night to honor Him and give

Him thanks. Always appreciate His presence, even if you cannot feel Him at the time. Rest assured, He is always there.

2. Send an invitation. When you receive an invitation to an event, you feel privileged and special. In your heart each day, send up a prayerful invite for the Lord to be with you each day. Ask Him for wisdom and strength on your daily journey.

3. Converse with Him. Tell Him your needs and concerns and ask for guidance. This doesn't have to be a long and drawn out chat. Just let Him know He is needed in your life. "And I tell you, ask, and it will be given to you; seek, and you will find; knock, and it will be opened to you" (Luke 11:9).

4. Listen. After you have asked and thanked Him for His blessings, step back and listen and wait. Your answer might come within minutes, hours, days, or months. Guests of Night to Shine look forward to their special event each year. Be patient and look forward to the answer God has for you. "Let the wise hear and increase in learning, and the one who understands obtain guidance" (Proverbs 1:5).

5. Praise Him. Everyone likes recognition. God created you and has provided for you, and better yet, He has prepared a place for you to spend eternity with Him if you choose. Thank Him and worship Him every day for this promise. "O Lord, you are my God; / I will exalt you; I will praise your name, / for you have done wonderful things, / plans formed of old, faithful for sure" (Isaiah 25:1).

The Night to Shine is so massive that it takes thousands of volunteers and months of planning to come together to produce a magical night. You can have this experience with the Lord every day without the hoopla and excessive planning. Make the Master the one who is made to feel like the King of the universe.

DAY 2
GOD'S PLAN WORKS

**José Altuve:
All-Star and MVP Second Baseman,
Houston Astros**

By Del Duduit

For I know the plans I have for you, declares the Lord, plans for welfare and not for evil, to give you a future and a hope.

—Jeremiah 29:11

To everyone who follows professional baseball, fans must think that José Altuve has it all.

The five-foot six-inch second baseman has captured several awards. His trophy case includes:

- Multiple All-Star honors
- A 2017 World Series Champion
- 2017 American League MVP
- 2019 American League Championship Series MVP
- A Gold Glove in 2015
- Several Silver Slugger Awards
- The Hank Aaron Award
- Multiple AL Batting Titles
- AL leader in stolen bases

You get the idea. The man can play baseball.

But he says his relationship with the Lord is more valuable than any honor that he has earned.

"My faith and my relationship with God just don't happen because I am successful. It just doesn't work that way," he said. "And I know that's easy for me to say because I'm playing in the majors, but I have gone through my share of struggles. But those don't stand out. What does stand out is that my mom and dad made sure we followed God. They lived the life, and we followed, because we saw how God took care of our family."

José was raised in a Christian family who believed Jesus is the Son of God and that the only way to heaven is to accept Him as Savior.

When he is on the road, José goes to chapel every Sunday and finds encouragement and strength in numbers.

"It's the way I was raised—to go to church and honor God," he said. "I have to stay focused on what He wants for me and what the Bible says. A lot of us [teammates] go to chapel together, and it's real. We talk to each other about how good God is to us, and it's something we all need."

Through all the good times and bad, José has stayed true to his upbringing.

He reads the Word of God and prays each day.

"It's what gives me strength," he said. "It's the main thing in my life."

To José, the relationship he has with the Lord is genuine.

"I really, really believe it," he added. "My faith is so important to me. I never want to step away from it, and I have no interest to know what life without God would be like."

> The heart of man plans his way,
> but the Lord establishes his steps.
>
> —Proverbs 16:9

José does not have a reason to give up on the grace of God. No one should. The Lord has been good to all of us.

Do you agree?

On Deck

You might not be a professional baseball player with a collection of awards, but you still have a reason to celebrate life. Maybe not everything has gone the way you planned, but you can look back and count your blessings. Have you lost sight of the fact that the Lord is the creator of the universe? Have minor aggravations crept into your life and formed gigantic problems? Has this caused you to slack off on the time you spend in prayer and in the Word of God?

Step Up to the Plate

You can never blame anyone else for your poor decisions. If you choose to stop reading the Bible or praying, it's no one else's fault but your own. God has not left and will always be on the throne. If you ever come to the place where you consider turning your back on God, remember what José said. "I never want to step away from it." That's because his faith works and is the only and best way to live. Here are some reasons to be thankful and blessed:

1. Life. If you are reading this book, you are alive. You breathe. Your heart beats. Whether you have all the riches this world can offer or you live in poverty, the most important thing is that your life is precious. Be thankful to God for His many blessings. "Then the Lord God formed the man of dust from the ground and breathed into his nostrils the breath of life, and the man became a living creature" (Genesis 2:7).

2. Family. Most people have loved ones who mean the world to them. You may have estranged relationships with family members, but you should love and pray for them anyway. Family is the backbone and foundation of the church. If you have a close family, work hard to continue the familiar traditions. If you did not enjoy a healthy family life growing up as a child, make sure you provide one for the family God blesses you with.

3. Friends. You might have thirty close friends or maybe just a couple. But if you can make lifetime memories with friends, you are rich beyond measure. Praise God for them. "That is, that we may be mutually encouraged by each other's faith, both yours and mine" (Romans 1:12).

4. Opportunities. When God opens doors, pray He will give you the courage to walk through them. Maybe He invites you to tell someone about Christ,

or He gives you a new job opportunity. Ask God for the wisdom to discern His will for your life and don't be afraid to answer His call.

5. Mistakes. Don't let slipups get you down or make you feel like a failure. Sometimes our best lessons come from the mistakes we make, and we learn the hard way not to make the same ones twice. Be thankful for these lessons God teaches you.

6. Basics. Your essential needs are food, shelter, clothing, income, love, mercy, and a home church. A BMW and a mansion are unnecessary wants. If you can earn enough money to buy them, that's fantastic. But be thankful for all the small blessings God gives you—He knows your needs better than you do. And follow His lead by being a blessing to others. "And my God will supply every need of yours according to his riches in glory in Christ Jesus" (Philippians 4:19).

José faced challenges and obstacles, but he also stayed faithful to what he learned as a child: to honor God, His Word, and His house. This lifestyle has worked for José, and he sees no reason to stray. He counts his blessings each day, and you can too. Stay close to the Master because His way is the best way.

DAY 3

WORK HARD WITH THE ABILITY GOD GIVES YOU

Francisco Lindor:
All-Star Shortstop,
Cleveland Indians

By Beckie Lindsey

Work willingly at whatever you do, as though you were working for the Lord rather than for people. Remember that the Lord will give you an inheritance as your reward, and that the Master you are serving is Christ.
—Colossians 3:23–24 NLT

"God gave me the ability and talent, but I had to work hard and practice with the talent He gave me."

No doubt about it, professional athletes make playing sports look easy. The average person watching a ballgame might even be led to believe the pros don't have to try hard at what they do—they were simply born with talent, which provided them with a shortcut to success.

All too often, we look for shortcuts—to success, weight loss, happiness, [fill in the blank]. The problem with shortcuts is that they're usually short-lived. When they don't pan out for us, we feel like throwing in the towel. But we need to endure physically, mentally, and spiritually in order to press on to achieve victory.

As the saying goes, "Life is a marathon, not a sprint." To run a marathon, you must train hard and persist. There are no shortcuts for the patience it takes to put in the effort.

You sure can try, but as J. R. R. Tolkien said, "Short cuts make long delays." The fact is, God didn't give special abilities to an elect few. He gave each of us spiritual gifts and talents He expects us to develop.

"It didn't just come to me; I had to work and prepare. I wanted to be good at my craft with the tools He gave me. I worked hard and stayed faithful to Him. If He would have wanted me to do something else, I would do it," Francisco said.

His work ethic, endurance, and faithfulness to develop his God-given talents won him the American League Rookie of the Month Award in September 2015, during which he batted .362. He finished that season with a .313 batting average, twelve home runs, fifty-one RBIs, twelve stolen bases, and twenty-two doubles over ninety-nine games for the Indians.

He also placed second for the American League Rookie of the Year Award. In 2016, Lindor earned his first World Series appearance as a member of the Indians, winners of the American League pennant.

Like Francisco, we need to come to terms with this fact: life is hard. Period. But this is not bad and is necessary to produce and accomplish. And these are good things, right? When one labors for the Lord, there is a sense of great satisfaction. Keep in mind, our good deeds do not earn our salvation, which is a free gift from God through Jesus Christ (Ephesians 2:8).

"Everyone has a talent to give. Everyone has hours to practice and pray. How hard are you going to work? That's up to you. I thank God for the talent He gave me," Francisco said. "If He gives you the talent to be an athlete or something else, then do it the best you can. Do it for His glory, and you will be happy."

When we make the decision to serve the Lord, we find happiness and joy in bringing honor and glory to Him. And that joy is evident to others, which in turn makes them desire what we have. We will find the kind of joy that gives us something to smile about like Francisco. "I have a reason to smile all the time. I have the love of God in my heart, and I can't help but smile. He makes me smile."

The same God who gave us our gifts and talents gives us what we need to grow if we make Him the center of our lives. His purpose is for us to grow physically, mentally, and spiritually to accomplish great things.

"My faith means everything to me. You have to believe in God and His Word. He has a plan for you—a purpose for you. He will help you accomplish great things," he said. "Just remember to always give Him the credit and the praise because if you don't, He might just take things away from you."

Now all glory to God, who is able, through his mighty power at work within us, to accomplish infinitely more than we might ask or think.

—Ephesians 3:20 NLT

On Deck

Our journey in life takes serious dedication and strength, but we are not alone. God Himself will help us. "By his divine power, God has given us everything we need for living a godly life" (2 Peter 1:3 NLT). The word for "power" used here is the Greek word *dunamis.* It is the root word of our English words *dynamite, dynamo,* and *dynamic.* In the first chapter of the Book of Ephesians, this power is said to be the same mighty power that raised Jesus from the dead (vv. 19–20)! This means we don't live the Christian life in our own power but in God's. In other words, we have dynamite power directly from Him available to us. If we determine to use the abilities God has given us, He supplies us with His power!

Step Up to the Plate

We must expect to put in the effort to experience God's power the same as Francisco. Try incorporating these steps:

1. Be thankful. Show appreciation to God for the abilities He has given you and all the many blessings in your life. Gratitude helps us stay positive and keep our focus on Him instead of ourselves. You may consider making a list of the blessings He has given you.
2. Ask for His direction. Many times we put our plans into action before asking God to direct them.

3. Make a commitment to spiritual strength and growth. Let's face it; we do the things we truly want to do. If we expect to grow as Christians, we must commit to do what it takes to make our spiritual lives a top priority.
4. Tell someone about your commitment. We all know the power of accountability. What better reason for accountability is there than spiritual growth?
5. Help someone. When we help others develop spiritually, it reinforces and multiplies our own growth.
6. Remember you are toiling for God. Our purpose is to always bring honor and glory to God. Try asking yourself at the end of each day, "How did I bring honor to God today?"

If you get tired of working hard, this is an indication you have moved away from one or more of the steps above. It's time to refocus on why we do the job in the first place and remember that this life is not all there is. When we've finished the game, a great inheritance awaits us.

DAY 4
IT'S NOT ABOUT ME

Michael Lorenzen:
Pitcher,
Cincinnati Reds

By Del Duduit

Not to us, Lord, not to us
but to your name be the glory,
because of your love and faithfulness.

—Psalm 115:1 NIV

"I want to praise Him in everything I do in life," Michael Lorenzen said. "In the small things and the big ones, I just want to give my God glory."

Professional baseball players, like most athletes, gather a lot of attention. They frequently appear on television, and their photos are seen on magazine covers and baseball cards. Thousands of people buy jerseys with their numbers on them. They hear their name chanted during games, and they are treated like royalty in some places.

Many are portrayed as larger than life and are idolized by children. When you are put on such a pedestal, it is difficult to maintain humility.

"I never want the fans to look at me and what I have done," Michael said. "If I do something and they applaud me, it's cool and all—I'm just doing my job. I appreciate them so much, but I want to give glory to God in everything."

When some players make a good play or rip a double down the right field fence, fans might see the athlete point to the sky or pound their chest in celebration.

Not Michael.

"I just try to have a not-look-at-me approach if I do something great on the field," he said. "Because in my eyes, then it becomes about me if I do that. That's just me."

Michael wants baseball fans who come to the game to enjoy themselves. He wants to perform well for the Reds and do his job.

He loves to play the game and gets satisfaction when he knows he has put forth the effort to help his team. But he also wants the people to see his work ethic and how he handles failure. He does not want to display anger on the field or shout a derogatory word.

"This is a game of failure," he said. "I just try to glorify God in all things. Am I happy when we lose? No. But I don't throw a fit or make a fool of myself. I want to inspire others when they see how I deal with failure."

Michael deals with disappointment by keeping a positive perspective. He is assured of salvation by the grace of God, which helps him find success in what he does on the field. "If you deny Him before man, He will deny us before the Father," Michael said. "That is why I want everyone to know I serve the Lord. I pitch for the Reds and I love it, but I serve the Lord."

Selfishness remains a big struggle among his peers. When players earn the kind of money they do, along with the five-star treatment, it's easy to see where they might become self-centered.

"We are put on a pedestal," he said. "We are in the limelight and everyone wants our autograph and to get a picture taken with them—and that's okay. I always have the mindset to use my platform to honor God."

And if a player likes the attention and wants to be noticed, that doesn't sit well with Michael. "Being a Christian means taking up your cross and following Christ," he said. "You have to deny yourself and live for Him."

Michael has done that so far. He gives God the glory for his personal accomplishments. He praises the Lord when he succeeds and when he fails.

"He's God no matter what," he said. "Being satisfied in that is all I need. Everything else really doesn't matter." He takes life in stride and applies biblical principles to everyday situations. He was the Reds' first-round draft pick in 2013, but he remains more thankful to be in God's lineup. "I am so grateful Cincinnati gave me this professional opportunity," he said. "But I am ever more thankful the Lord saved me, and that's why I give Him glory all the time. It's not about me."

> In the same way, let your light shine before others, that they may see your good deeds and glorify your Father in heaven.
>
> —Matthew 5:16 NIV

On Deck

You might hold an important job or position in the community. People might recognize you on every street corner and want to shake your hand. How do you deal with that? Do you gloat, or are you humble? Remember, you could lose it all any day. Be grateful you have a good job and friends. Never take this for granted or ignore people. On the other hand, you may find yourself in the opposite camp and feel like just another number. Maybe you get lost in the shuffle of life and no one knows who you are. Always remember God cares for you. If He cares enough to feed the sparrow, he will take care of you. In either case, glorify God and honor Him—whether you are in the starting lineup or coming off the bench.

Step Up to the Plate

For some, modesty does not come naturally. Your first move is to ask God for a humble spirit. Now that you want to be that way, here are seven ways to show humility.

1. Ask for feedback. If you ask, you will receive. Be prepared for an answer you might not want to hear. Honest advice from others is a great way to help improve yourself.
2. Don't assume everyone likes what you do. Be proud of your strengths but acknowledge your weaknesses and work to improve on them.
3. Confront your prejudices. If you portray negative views about something or someone, do your research and make an informed decision. Look for similarities rather than differences.
4. Ask a question. This can lead to fantastic discussions and show others you still have more to learn. You

don't have all the answers. Be honest and don't pretend to be an expert on all topics. People find it refreshing when you ask them a question about their area of interest or expertise instead of talking about yourself.

5. Listen. This might be a hard one. Don't plan on what you want to say before a person is finished talking to you. Listen to people while they speak to you. They will appreciate and notice when you take a genuine interest. You don't need to counter with a larger story that minimizes their experience.

6. Accept setback. Humility allows you to accept challenges even when you know they could potentially lead to failure. If something doesn't turn out as expected, then you learn from it. A setback provides another opportunity for success. Make the changes and go forward. "Do nothing out of selfish ambition or vain conceit. Rather, in humility value others above yourselves" (Philippians 2:3 NIV).

7. Discover awe. When you are humble, you are aware you are not the most important person in the world. Look up at the stars at night or offer your arm to an elderly person who needs help down the stairs. Take note you are one person in the world among billions. You are important, but you are not the most important. Recognize you are God's creation, and He will take care of you. "Pride brings a person low, / but the lowly in spirit gain honor" (Proverbs 29:23 NIV). If God makes you feel special, who else do you need?

Do your job and do it well. Honor the Lord's name and recognize He is the reason you do what you can—and praise Him always. When you realize that the life God has blessed you with is NOT about you, but about Him, then you can begin to prioritize things in the correct manner.

DAY 5

MAKE IT A POINT TO INSPIRE HOPE

Clayton Kershaw:
Multiple Cy Young Award–Winning Pitcher,
Los Angeles Dodgers

By Clint Rutledge

May the God of hope fill you with all joy and peace as you trust in him, so that you may overflow with hope by the power of the Holy Spirit.

—Romans 15:13 NIV

Clayton Kershaw is a self-proclaimed cookie guy. "I can crush the cookies," he says. His favorite movie is *Dumb and Dumber,* his favorite color is green, his favorite practice drill is pepper, his favorite subject in school was English, and his favorite thing to do in the lives of others is to instill hope.

You know hope—it has a way of showing up at times when you need it most. Your bank account is low, but there is that one deal that is on its way.

Your favorite team is down by one point, but there is still some time left on the clock. The doctor gives you news you don't want to hear but says he knows what to do to make everything okay. We need hope almost as much as we need water, food, and air.

When good news comes your way, hope gets stronger. When bad news comes your way, you immediately start looking for hope. If you are a kid at Christmas, hope shows up every time you look under the tree. If you are a grandparent, it shows up when you think about the entire family getting together. Hope is free to possess but devastating to lose.

Clayton and his wife, Ellen, met hope one day. They met it in the form of something they could give, something they wished for, and they met hope in the form of a little girl. Hope was born in Lusaka, Zambia, and she had battled HIV her entire life. She was an orphan who was sick and abused, and she was in need of what her name suggested.

The couple realized God had put them in a position to provide hope to a little girl named Hope, and this was when Kershaw's Challenge was born. The two were heartbroken by the depth of poverty in Lusaka, and they began to pray about how God could use them to make a difference.

God gave them the opportunity to provide a place for Hope and many other kids in Zambia to get a good meal, a good night's sleep, and a quality education.

In December 2012, they opened Arise Home. For the first time, eight kids (including Hope) had their own beds to sleep in and loving housemothers to tuck them in at night. In 2016, thanks to many donors, a second home was opened. Kershaw's Challenge is now doing great work in the lives of children not only in Zambia but also in Los Angeles, Dallas, and the Dominican Republic. Clayton knows his ability to throw a baseball is given by God, and it is meant for him to use his talent to bless others.

"Baseball is a gift. It is a way we can give back to help those in need," he said. "Because of baseball, we are blessed with a lot of exposure, and therefore, we have a platform to bring attention to the needs of others."

The group's website states the nonprofit is a "faith-based, others-focused organization. We exist to encourage people to use whatever God-given passion or talent they have to make a difference and give back to people in need. We want to empower people to use their spheres of influence to impact communities positively and to expand God's Kingdom."

Hope showed up in many ways the day Clayton and Ellen met a little girl in Lusaka, Zambia. Hope was shown to be a real person, but she also symbolized a real need— one God put right in front of them. To their credit, they opened their hearts to God's guidance and allowed Him to work through them.

> For everything that was written in the past was written to teach us, so that through the endurance taught in the Scriptures and the encouragement they provide we might have hope.
>
> —Romans 15:4 NIV

On Deck

What about you? Has God placed the needs of others right in front of you? You don't have to be a major league pitcher to make a major league difference. Where is God calling you to help someone near you? Your challenge today is to meet Kershaw's Challenge. Find someone to help in your sphere of influence or in your community and then see what amazing things God will do in and through you. Just like Clayton and Ellen, you might just find that Hope comes in many forms, and it always shows up when you need it the most.

Step Up to the Plate

How can you inspire those in your circle or on your team?

1. Show you care. Simple phrases like "How are you today?" or "Have a great afternoon" are fine, but they are often said out of routine. Instead, take a vested interest in someone's life and invite that person for coffee. Spend time with them, listen, and offer a solution to a problem they may have. "Do not merely look out for your own personal interests, but also for the interests of others" (Philippians 2:4 NASB).

2. Stay positive. This can be tough at times, especially when there might be a sad situation. But recognize the moment and share the light and be an encouragement. If someone insults you, find a way to spin the remark and make others smile. If someone is upset about a job loss or a breakup, try to find a silver lining. "Rejoice in hope, be patient in tribulation, be constant in prayer" (Romans 12:12).

3. Speak life into others. This can be done in private and in prayer. When you are one-on-one with someone, find a good quality and tell them. Also

let them know you will remember them and their situation in prayer. "First of all, then, I urge that supplications, prayers, intercessions, and thanksgivings be made for all people" (1 Timothy 2:1). Most of the time, a friend just needs to know you talk to the Father on their behalf.

When you put others first, you will become an encourager and a beacon of hope. These are rare qualities. In comparison, it's like winning the Cy Young Award—it's only given out to the best.

DAY 6
YOU CAN BE ANYTHING YOU WANT

Albert Pujols:
Multiple MVP Winner and First Baseman,
Los Angeles Angels of Anaheim

By Del Duduit

I can do all things through Christ which strengtheneth me.
—Philippians 4:13 KJV

"Sometimes, you might hear that you'll never be able to accomplish something you want," Albert Pujols said. "In God's eyes, we will be anything He wants us to be. We just have to accept the plan."

Sometimes accepting what the Lord has for you may be frustrating. Perhaps He wants you to do something you never considered or even liked. Maybe you have no experience.

My friend George worked in the financial markets for thirty years. Business was all he knew. But one day, he felt the Lord leading him to start up a Christian-based professional racing team. At the time, he had no knowledge of the sport and did not follow racing. But George listened to God's voice and did what He said, and he now has a wonderful ministry through the platform of professional automobile racing.

In biblical days, Noah must have wondered the same thing. He must have questioned the Lord a few times, especially when the crowd began to laugh and mock him.

But Noah listened, and we all know what happened.

Many kids who are baseball fans today admire Albert. After all, he has earned respect from anyone who knows anything about the sport.

He is a decorated player who will see his name enshrined in the National Baseball Hall of Fame and Museum in Cooperstown, New York, when he retires.

As a kid growing up in Santo Domingo, Dominican Republic, the sport was a big part of his childhood. He was an only child, and his grandmother played a big role in his upbringing. His father was a softball pitcher and an alcoholic.

There were times when Albert had to help take his drunk father home after a game. He liked baseball, using cut-up milk cartons for gloves and limes as baseballs. He enjoyed hitting as much as he could as a youngster.

In 1996, his family moved to New York City where he soon witnessed a shooting. Two years later, he and his family were off to Missouri to live with relatives. He found his place on the high school baseball team, and his reputation began to spread.

Then in 1998, he was off to Maple Woods Community College where he smacked a grand slam and turned a rare unassisted triple play in his first game. Destiny was written all over him. Although he was not a Christian at the time, God had plans for Albert. "Growing up, I never really expected to be where I am today, but God gets all the glory," he said. "It just goes to show that you have to let the Lord develop you into what He wants."

His message to young adults and teenagers is simple: Listen to the Lord and go where He leads you. "If you want to be a baseball player, then the Lord will pave a way," he said. "If God doesn't want you to play baseball and you think you can, God will shut the doors."

Albert is a constant encourager. He instructs youth not to take their signals from people but instead to take guidance from the Lord. "There are many times in life people might tell you that you can't do something like play ball," he said. "In God's eyes, we can do anything—especially if He wants us to. We are His creation and His image, so don't let anyone tell you any different." He believes you are put in a situation for a specific reason: to glorify the Lord. "Wherever God puts you, take every single opportunity to thank and praise Him."

> Praise ye the Lord. Praise God in his sanctuary: praise him in the firmament of his power.
>
> —Psalm 150:1 KJV

On Deck

You might be struggling with making a decision at work or deciding your major in college. You might be in a job you don't like and feel a calling to completely change and go in a different direction. Will you be like George who went completely out of his element and changed careers? This can be a frightening time. Is God calling you to action, or are you hearing what you want to hear from the Lord? Are you merely convincing yourself you hear Him to justify your decision? Ask God to give you wisdom and discernment to be able to tell the difference.

Step Up to the Plate

Being what God wants you to be can be wonderful, but you may become intimidated on the way to fulfilling His plan for your life. Trust God to make you what He wants you to be as you remember to do the following:

1. Recognize the Lord has created you to be special. You are His, and He will not turn his back on you. Especially remember He is by your side as you make life-changing decisions.
2. Align your decisions with God's will for your life. Are your own motives getting in the way? Is your plan what you want or what the Lord wants? You need deep soul searching and prayer in order to find the true answer. This can be tough to do at times, because you might have your own goals in mind. But God's plans are always best even when they are different from our dreams. Accept His game strategy for your life with humility.
3. Make sure you dedicate sufficient time to spend in prayer. Gratitude and praise should be at the top of your list of priorities. Listen and wait patiently for God to answer. He might just be waiting for you to first give Him praise. Ask and believe and be mindful of the Holy Spirit's leading in your life.

4. Focus on the Word of God and ask the Lord to reveal His plan to you through Scripture. Read and study faithfully every day and meditate alone with God in a quiet area as you patiently wait for His answers and allow Him to speak to you. Invite the Holy Spirit to refresh your mind anew every day.

5. Don't try to pull a squeeze play in an attempt to force or persuade God to approve your plan. Bargaining is not an option. There are no dealmakers in God's family. "Wait for the Lord; / be strong and take heart / and wait for the Lord" (Psalm 27:14 NIV).

6. Know and recognize God's voice. He speaks with authority, but His voice brings peace. Satan is the author of confusion, so if you're getting mixed signals, rebuke the devil, and ask God to give you clarity and confirmation. "My sheep hear my voice, and I know them, and they follow me" (John 10:27 KJV).

7. Have the courage to trust God's plan for your life. He will not call you to do something He does not equip you to do. Believe in His timing, and accept the challenges He gives you, knowing He is with you all the way.

The best advice from Albert is to believe the Lord will guide you and open the doors to success in whatever He chooses. But the last two words are so crucial—you can be anything you want in the Lord, when He chooses.

DAY 7
IMPACTING THE NEXT GENERATION

Andrew McCutchen:
Outfielder,
New York Yankees
and Former National League MVP

By Ryan Farr

Start children off on the way they should go,
and even when they are old they will not turn from it.
—Proverbs 22:6 NIV

Have you ever watched a Little League baseball practice? Talk about a change of perspective and pace. Watching kids working the basic fundamentals of a game because it's what they enjoy doing . . . no commercials, no selfish ambition, and no contacts. It is just pure innocent love of the sport of baseball. At this level it's less about being elite at the sport and more about how the sport is shaping each of those young lives. And who does the shaping? Ask the man with the clipboard.

Typically, he is a volunteer father and rarely an expert in the game. He coaches because he loves his kids and wants them to have a great experience. He may seem low on the coaching totem pole compared to high school and college play-callers, but the influence he has is significant.

How he responds in each and every situation on the field will impact his young players for a lifetime. Every encouraging word must be measured, each seemingly simple gesture regarded, and any correction delivered carefully. It's a tough job but an essential one.

Young people are impressionable, and we should never take for granted an opportunity to impact them for the better! Andrew McCutchen, five-time MLB All-Star and current outfielder for the New York Yankees, discusses this very important concept of influencing the next generation.

And this isn't just a lesson for the baseball diamond. Being a positive role model lends itself to life and our walk with Christ. "Kids today need to find a good mentor," he says. "They need someone who can tell them what it is they need to do—things they need to believe in and things they need to trust." Just like a young pitcher learning his footwork or an inexperienced batter learning the proper technique for his swing, young people need to learn about God's desires for their lives and His promise to stick by them through the ups and the downs.

A player like Andrew McCutchen knows what it's like to be a young athlete looking up to the big leaguers, but now he also has the privilege of being one who is looked up to by thousands of young baseball fans. This role is one he does not take lightly and certainly hopes to succeed at. Why? Because he knows where a lack of direction can lead in a person's life "If you are a kid who does not have a mentor, you are a dog without a leash," says Andrew. "You need [direction] on a daily basis. Encourage [young people] to find a good spiritual mentor who can lead [them] in the right direction, and that is God."

Who in your life needs a spiritual coach? Maybe they are someone younger who looks up to an adult to show them what it means to live out their faith on a daily basis. Maybe they are not young in age but are spiritually immature and need someone who has walked the valleys of life with Christ leading the way to show them an example of true surrender. Whatever the case may be, don't relegate yourself to the stands and wait for someone else to step in. Grab your clipboard and Bible, coach, and go make a difference!

> You are the salt of the earth; but if the salt has become tasteless, how can it be made salty again? It is no longer good for anything, except to be thrown out and trampled under foot by men. You are the light of the world. A city set on a hill cannot be hidden; nor does anyone light a lamp and put it under a basket, but on the lampstand, and it gives light to all who are in the house.
>
> —Matthew 5:13–15 NASB

On Deck

Consider the people God has placed in your life. Perhaps you know a young person who would benefit from hearing your testimony and what God has taught you personally through trials and struggles. Maybe you know someone who isn't young in age but is new in their walk with Christ. They may be in need of someone to be a spiritual mentor and, instead of assuming this job will fall on the shoulders of another, God may be calling you. Whatever the case may be, God has called his sons and daughters to be mentors and examples to the next generation. How are you contributing to that call today?

Step Up to the Plate

Write out your testimony, a brief description about how God has influenced your life and transformed you for the better. Take a night to read it back over and say a prayer of thanks to God for how He has led you.

Once you have done that, make a list of five people God has placed in your life to influence. They can be a family member, friend, coworker, classmate, or someone you encounter daily. Now consider ways you could share part of your testimony with them. Now this doesn't mean that you have to invite them out to coffee and dump the entire story on them at one time. But maybe there are parts of your journey that relate to what they are going through and God might be desiring to speak to them through your words.

My Testimony:
Who in my life can I impact?
Name:
Name:
Name:
Name:
Name:

Sometimes it can be difficult for us to share our story and our faith. It may require us to get out of our comfort zone and share at a level we never have with someone close to us.

But be encouraged. The same God who called us to "go and make disciples of all the nations" also gave us a promise: "And surely I am with you always, to the very end of the age" (Matthew 28:19–20 NIV). You are not alone. Step up to the plate and make a difference. Impact five people and ask each one to do the same. What a difference that could make.

DAY 8

PUT ASIDE THE EGO

Brian Dozier:
All-Star Second Baseman,
Washington Nationals

By Del Duduit

Do you not know that your bodies are temples of the Holy
Spirit, who is in you, whom you have received from God?
You are not your own.

—1 Corinthians 6:19 NIV

"When you truly devote yourself to Jesus and do what He
says, great things will happen in your life," Brian Dozier
told me. It's easy to profess Christianity in church where
you are in a safe environment. But when it's time to put
your faith to the test, are you really willing to do what God
asks you to do? Are you prepared to put aside your own
wants and your ego to live according to God's will?

In baseball, fundamentals are preached in order to be
successful. Most Sundays after attending church and
watching some NASCAR, Brian's dad took him to the park
to teach him to field grounders the right way. But instead
of using a glove, Brian used wooden paddles, which taught
him the correct technique—to stay low, keep his eye on the
ball, and always use both hands.

"As a player, if you don't have those basic fundamental skills, it will show right away," he said. Likewise, fundamentals are necessary to be a successful Christian. You may be expected to attend church and pay your tithes. But an important part of your walk includes glorifying God and realizing your purpose. "I can praise the Lord in times of struggles," he said. "When you can honestly give Him glory and praise when things don't go as planned, and not expect anything in return, then you are grounded."

He is living out his dream now, but life has not always gone his way. In 2011, the Minnesota Twins named him Minor League Player of the Year.

The outlook appeared bright for the future All-Star when he got a call promoting him to the big leagues. He played shortstop on the biggest stage in baseball, and his professional dreams were coming true. But these dreams became nightmares halfway into the season. Although he had played the same position since childhood, he struggled a great deal, and the team sent him back to the minors.

"This game is about failure and how you deal with it," he said. "I had always heard that it's tough to get to the majors and even tougher to stay. I found that out." The team gave him another chance, but it came with a choice. If he wanted to play in the Twin City, he must switch positions and move to second base. There is a vast difference between playing shortstop and second base. Mainly it's the angles. At shortstop, you see the entire infield. At second base, you are limited and must learn to pivot, especially when executing the crucial and important double play. "At second base, there will be guys sliding into me just to put me on the ground," he said. "They try to take my legs out, and I can't see them sometimes. I just have to feel them."

He put aside his ego and did the best thing for the team. He accepted the change and got better as a result. He met the challenge head-on and learned every aspect of his new role. He changed his footwork along with his throwing angles, learned how to turn the double play another way, and learned how to cover first base at times.

"I wanted to be the best second baseman I could be," he said. "There were some adjustments to make, but after I got comfortable, I really took off."

This was an understatement.

He established a franchise record for the most home runs by a second baseman while committing the fewest errors. He found his place. He returned to the majors and led the team in runs scored (72), RBIs (66), and home runs (18). The 2013 season marked a drastic difference to the previous one.

He worked hard and applied his fundamental teachings in order to be a success. Each year his stat line improved. In 2014, he blasted 23 home runs, drove in 71 runs, and scored 112 times. The same holds true spiritually. You do not always anticipate Satan throwing problems at you, wanting to take you down to the ground. You must be ready at all times and let God take care of these attacks when you can't.

You should pivot, look at the target, make the throw, and get out of the way. Let God make the play. "This is not just about following Him," Brian said. "It's not about living your life with God on the backburner. When you give yourself totally to Him and let Him direct your life, then it will be a whole lot easier."

> Blessed is the one
> who trusts in the Lord,
> who does not look to the proud,
> to those who turn aside to false gods.
>
> —Psalm 40:4 NIV

On Deck

You might be going through a situation like Brian's story about his demotion. It's a shot to the ego and might make a mess of your expectations. Prepare yourself by being fundamentally sound in the Word of God. Be willing to put aside your ego and pride and take a similar approach to what he did to save his job. It turned out to be the best move he ever made. Be willing to listen to others at times and take the necessary steps to achieve spiritual success. Lead your team and commit fewer errors.

Step Up to the Plate

There are ways to put your ego in check and sell out for the Lord.

1. Realize the importance of others. Once you master this, your life will change. Put others first and help them out. Humility shows strength and attracts attention and admiration. Demonstrate love and

compassion by volunteering at a homeless shelter or taking food to a needy family.

2. A sense of humor can do wonders for your self-esteem, and it can also dramatically impact those around you. You are not expected to be the next Jerry Seinfeld, but you can be happy. Lighten up and laugh at yourself. "A cheerful heart is good medicine, / but a crushed spirit dries up the bones" (Proverbs 17:22 NIV).

3. Recognize you are where you are due to God's grace. You may study hard to pass a test or work long hours to close a deal, but ultimately God gives you the ability and talent. Be ready to do whatever the Lord wants. You may work toward a goal for years, but the Lord guides you in the opposite direction. Brian told me he's fully prepared to stop playing baseball if the Lord leads him another way. "I'm fine with that," he said. "And I love having that feeling because I know He will take care of me."

4. Spend time in the Word of God, the best way to connect and find what the Lord wants from you. Humble yourself before the Lord, and He will exalt you.

Brian humbled himself and learned another position. Instead of quitting, he worked harder and performed better. Do what the team needs and not what you desire. Don't make any errors and make the effort to learn different angles. You will become better each year.

DAY 9

THE STRUGGLE WITH SIN

R. A. Dickey:
Cy Young Award–Winning Pitcher,
Atlanta Braves

By Cyle Young

Thus says the Lord:

> "Let not the wise man glory in his wisdom,
> Let not the mighty man glory in his might,
> Nor let the rich man glory in his riches;
> But let him who glories glory in this,
> That he understands and knows Me,
> That I am the Lord, exercising lovingkindness, judgment,
> and righteousness in the earth.
> For in these I delight," says the Lord.
>
> —Jeremiah 9:23–24 NKJV

Pitcher R. A. Dickey represented the United States at the 1996 Olympics in Atlanta. He started two games, and Team USA won both and secured the bronze medal. Along with his Olympic medal, R. A.'s twenty-two-year career in Major League Baseball spanned six different franchises, and he accrued 120 wins and 1,477 strikeouts.

The Nashville, Tennessee, native has always tried to keep a proper perspective on his place in the world. As a famous athlete, he looks to his favorite Bible verses, Jeremiah 9:23–24, to guide his thoughts and behavior. He doesn't take glory in his pitches.

Instead, he focuses on understanding and knowing Jesus Christ as Lord of his life. "Giving back is so important to me. I want to demonstrate and pour into other people," he said. Nothing exemplifies this mindset more than his focus on the nonprofit ministry he helps operate in Ocala, Florida.

Honoring the Father Ministries donates baseball equipment, medical supplies, and powdered milk to impoverished families and communities in Latin America. R. A. also strives to live his life in such a way that people see Christ reflected through his actions, attitude, and behavior.

He believes people might notice "how I love on my teammates, how I respond to adversity, and the things I do with my life apart from baseball," he said. His sincere hope is that his lifestyle draws people into the saving grace of Jesus. He is quick to share the value of each individual person. "From the ticket taker at the game to the security guard, the bat boy, or the fans—we are all the same." Every person has value, and they should all be treated with respect, he noted.

And as you wish that others would do to you, do so to them.

—Luke 6:31

When R. A. looks at the Gospels, he resonates the most with John. He relates to John's story, and he loves the humility he sees in him, especially because John had every reason to be proud—he was one of Jesus closest friends. But R. A. loves that John "walked gently." Being a professional athlete means there is always a spotlight on you. R. A. said, "My role as a player is a responsibility more than anything else. I'm looked at daily in the media and by fans."

People are always watching, and he believes they will gain more from seeing a good sermon than just hearing one, because actions always speak louder than words. "If people can see the Lord in the things I do or say, then they are seeing a good sermon."

On Deck

What a great example to follow. R. A. has the proper perspective on life, and you can too. Remember to be humble and to walk gently through life; avoid pride and treat others with respect. Find someone who lives with the character and behavior you want to emulate and then try to learn from them. R. A. looked up to an uncle who was instrumental in his faith, loved him well, and helped him to grow as a person and an athlete. Reach out to someone in your family or church who can pour the love of Jesus into your life.

Step Up to the Plate

Do you want your life to reflect Christ? Would you rather live a good sermon than try to preach one with just empty words? You can do this with only a few adjustments to your daily routine. Apply these steps below, and you will be well on your way to living a life that values others more than yourself:

1. Pray and ask God to give you a desire to love others. Mankind is innately selfish. This is hardwired into our broken world as a result of original sin and the fall of man. But selfishness doesn't have to control you or define you, and God can help you overcome those greedy desires of your heart.

2. Treat others with respect. This may seem like an easy task, but it isn't. Our society doesn't value each person equally, and this negative influence impacts, models, and shapes our thoughts. To treat others with respect, you have to choose to value another person. This not a natural instinct. It is an intentional decision.

3. Walk gently. Don't brag or boast. Live your life and enjoy it, but no one in the world needs to find you standing on a street corner holding a megaphone proclaiming how awesome you are to the ends of the earth. When you walk gently, you are content with living your life with quiet humility. You can enjoy your successes but take joy in knowing God sees your good deeds. He delights in you and your successes, and this should be sufficient for you.

4. Grow in Christ. R. A.'s favorite verse in Jeremiah talks about how important it is to know and understand the Lord. Spend time studying God's Word. Nourish God-honoring relationships with other believers who can help you grow deeper in

love with Jesus. Life will get tough at times, and in these moments, it's important to have your heavenly Father walking gently through life beside you.

Don't make life too complicated. When you do the little things on a daily basis, it will feel like you've hit a grand slam to win the game at the end of each day.

DAY 10
PRAISE AWAY THE DEVIL'S ATTACKS

Robinson Chirinos:
Catcher,
Houston Astros

By Del Duduit

the Lord opens the eyes of the blind.
The Lord lifts up those who are bowed down;
the Lord loves the righteous.

—Psalm 146:8

On the morning of March 11, 2012, Robinson Chirinos made the bold decision to follow God.

Later that afternoon, he suffered a concussion after he was struck in the facemask by a foul ball.

The forces of evil did not like the choice he made and wanted to make it clear they were not happy.

But Robinson was.

"I felt so good that morning because I cried out to God in my heart," he said. "I felt Him so close that morning, then I had the concussion in the game that afternoon."

God and Robinson communed together in the early hours on that day. It was real.

"It wasn't like other people were talking to me about God," he said. "It was God. It was Him. I'll never forget it."

The knock to the head turned into an ordeal that caused him to miss the rest of the season. He suffered constant headaches and was nauseated and dizzy for several months. He couldn't shake it.

And he also dealt with anxiety because the devil whispered in his ear that his career was over.

"I didn't sleep much at all—maybe two hours each night," he said. "I stayed in my apartment most of the time."

A medical expert who specializes in concussions met with Robinson, and that started the healing process.

"I knew I was under attack from the very beginning," he added. "It was a tough time in my life. My whole world was turned upside down. I didn't know if I'd ever play ball again. It was crazy, but I know God brought me through. I could not have made it without Him."

That experience made Robinson a stronger Christian. He spent hours each day in prayer getting closer to the Master.

"I grew up knowing there was a God but didn't have a relationship with Him—nothing—until that day," he said. "I grow every day, and I feel more comfortable with Him, and my faith grows too. He's been too good to me."

> And Jesus said to him, "'If you can'! All things are possible for one who believes."
>
> —Mark 9:23

Are you strong enough spiritually to withstand the attacks of the enemy? Have you come under fire for your faith?

On Deck

The devil never plays fair. Maybe you have been a target of the forces of evil for taking a stand and proclaiming Christ. Perhaps you raised your hands in praise at church, and the next day you experienced car trouble. Or maybe you witnessed to a coworker about the goodness of the Lord, and the next day you suffered a personal setback. Satan wants you to back down. He uses tactics that are diabolical and plans your demise. Robinson made the choice to accept Jesus into his heart, and later that day, he went on a long journey of uncertainty. But he stayed close to the Savior.

Step Up to the Plate

If you are a child of God, you will come under fire at some point in your life. This does not mean you are not living for His glory. Once you make a confession of faith, you place a target on your back for the devil to shoot at. His plan is to make you want to give up and quit. Here are some steps to consider when you have been struck in the face by a fast ball:

1. Stay in the Word. Never let the devil tell you that you are worthless or that God cannot protect you. Rely on God's truth and stand firm on His Word. The battle is won through the promises of scripture. Satan might think he has you down, so memorize some verses and use them to respond to his accusations. "For by grace you have been saved

through faith. And this is not your own doing; it is the gift of God, not a result of works, so that no one may boast" (Ephesians 2:8–9).

2. Testify more. This will strengthen you in times of struggle. If a player is in a slump, he might spend some extra time in the batting cages or watching film to help him improve his game. When you tell your story to others, it gives you much needed power from heaven. "Come and hear, all you who fear God, / and I will tell what he has done for my soul" (Psalm 66:16).

3. Remember your salvation experience. Don't live in the past, but remember when you started your spiritual journey. God sent His Son to die for you so you can have eternal life in glory. Think back to that blessed day when His Holy Spirit came into your heart and set you free from the chains of sin. Ask Him to renew you afresh every day and draw you closer to Him.

4. Invest in your prayer life. When you are under attack, set your clock to get up earlier so you can spend some extra time in prayer to fight off the enemy. Speak the precious name of Jesus and use it to rebuke Satan's attempts to bring you down and destroy you. Begin your prayer with thanksgiving and praise for all of His blessings on your life.

5. Praise God. The best way to knock the devil out of the game is to stand and praise God and give Him glory for all your blessings. Praise Him for all the things He has done for you and for all the

things He kept you from. "I will sing of the Lord's great love forever; / with my mouth I will make your faithfulness known / through all generations. / I will declare that your love stands firm forever" (Psalm 89:1–2 NIV).

Believers are not exempt from tough times, but we have the best source of power to deal with life's struggles and challenges. Robinson faced some dark days, but he stayed close to the Lord. Now when he goes about his daily life, he uses the breastplate of righteousness as his chest protector and the helmet of salvation as his mask. Make sure you are ready to deflect the wild pitches and foul balls caused by the enemy.

DAY 11
YOU ARE ONE OF A KIND TO GOD

Adam Cimber:
Pitcher,
Cleveland Indians

By Del Duduit

I praise you, for I am fearfully and wonderfully made.
Wonderful are your works; my soul knows it very well.
—Psalm 139:14

When Adam Cimber was fourteen years old, he wasn't that big in stature.

He loved to pitch, but he soon discovered that his size made it difficult for him to put much heat behind his throws from the mound.

If he tried to fire a fastball, the batter would surely blast it over the fence. He had a dilemma. "I couldn't throw that hard," Adam said. "I was little and didn't have too many options."

His father pondered, then tossed in his two cents and developed a scheme that might work.

"My dad said if I wanted to make the high school team, I needed to do something different," he said. "We watched some videos of Oakland's Brad Ziegler and copied his style."

Ziegler had an uncanny submarine style delivery that made batters feel uncomfortable, and they had trouble picking up the ball after it was released.

Since Adam was "skinny," the method was perfect for his frame and build.

He made the team at Puyallup High School in Washington and soon caught the eyes of college scouts.

Adam enrolled at the University of Washington and played baseball from 2010 to 2012, posting a record of 4-6 with a 3.30 ERA. He then transferred to the University of San Francisco where he went 6-3 with an ERA of 3.74.

In 2013, the San Diego Padres drafted Adam in the ninth round of the 2013 MLB draft. He made the opening-day roster and debuted on the mound on March 29, 2018.

He was traded to Cleveland the next season and posted a 6-3 record in 2019 with an ERA of 4.45 and added 41 strike outs.

Adam's unique style provides the batter with a different and unusual look because there is a contrasting release point, and the ball moves in a peculiar way.

"[Hitters] are not used to this style, and it takes them a while to figure it out," Adam added. "That's the advantage. We had to come up with something different to offset the lack of speed."

When Adam steps to the mound, his opponents are aware of his unique throwing style. They study his motions and delivery but still have issues at the plate. The ball moves funny, and it's not what they are used to seeing from most pitchers.

For we are his workmanship, created in Christ Jesus for good works, which God prepared beforehand, that we should walk in them.

—Ephesians 2:10

On Deck

The devil does not care if you are a young up-and-coming star in the faith or if you are a veteran all-star in the church. He wants to strike you out and leave you demoralized. He will not play by the rules. He will throw low and inside and try to make you chase the pitch. Then he will fire a fastball at the corner before he eventually throws at your head. He is relentless and will use every pitch in his arsenal to make you go down on strikes. In life, he might cause you to lose your job at the worst time, or he could send in moral temptations to ruin a relationship and damage your reputation. Whenever challenges come to Adam, whether he is on the mound or at home, he relies on scripture to get him through a tough time.

"I always have that to come back to when a unique obstacle comes my way," he said. "I also love to serve my fellow man—that is a unique delivery, and I focus on others, and that helps me get through things and it helps to show others that God lives in you."

Step Up to the Plate

Adam said he likes to depend on the Word of God when he is confronted with a trial. The devil will tell you that you do not matter. He will whisper in your ear that God is not real and cannot help you. He will do his best to send the demons of discouragement into the dugout and surround you with doubt and confusion. It doesn't matter if you face a financial struggle, health issues, or a moral conflict, the devil wants you to lose. When you make the call to the bullpen of scripture, you will have the advantage over the devil's most powerful hitter. Here are some game-saving verses to commit to memory when you are called to the mound with the game on the line to empower you and let you know you are a unique child of God.

1. "Before I formed you in the womb I knew you, / and before you were born I consecrated you; / I appointed you a prophet to the nations" (Jeremiah 1:5). God knows everything that is worth knowing. You don't have all the answers, and when you are faced with a decision, call on the Lord for His guidance. After all, He knows what is best for you because He made you.

2. "But even the hairs of your head are all numbered" (Matthew 10:30). Christ cares so much for you that He is aware of every aspect of His creation. This also applies if you are bald—so don't worry if you fall into this category. The point is that the Master created you in a unique and awesome manner. You are one of a kind.

3. "Now you are the body of Christ and individually members of it" (1 Corinthians 12:27). When you become a Christian, you become a member of a

different society. You have a direct line to Christ and can always call on Him. You are unique.

4. "I can do all things through him who strengthens me" (Philippians 4:13). When you claim this verse as your own, you will be equipped to share the gospel of Christ to a lost and dying world. You can persevere and find your way through struggles. You are unique.

5. "But God shows his love for us in that while we were still sinners, Christ died for us" (Romans 5:8). Never allow the devil or anyone else to tell you that you are not important. This scripture tells the entire story in eighteen words. God loved you so much that He sent His son to die for you and your sins. You are unique.

"In this game, you constantly get knocked down, then you get lifted up and get knocked down," Adam said. "This is just where God has put me to work, and I'm going to work for Him." Adam knows that it doesn't matter if he's having a good or bad day on the field, he knows he is working for the kingdom of God. He is assured that he is one of God's children, and that makes him as unique as his unconventional delivery method. "People watch and see how I act, and I have to show them God in everything I do." Adam is unique and rare in the sight of the Master— and so are you.

DAY 12
UNDERSTAND GOD LOVES YOU

Chris Davis:
All-Star First Baseman,
Baltimore Orioles

By Del Duduit

> For God so loved the world, that he gave his only begotten
> Son, that whosoever believeth in him should not perish,
> but have everlasting life.
>
> —John 3:16 KJV

Chris Davis was six years old when he gave his life to Jesus
Christ. He was baptized in the Baptist Church in Longview,
Texas, and he had a good life while he was growing up.

While attending Longview High School, he played
shortstop and pitched. He was selected by the New York
Yankees in the 2004 MLB draft but declined to join the
organization. Instead, he went to Navarro Junior College
in Texas where he played first and third base.

After he turned down a draft from the Los Angeles
Angels of Anaheim in 2005, he was named the preseason
junior college All-American.

In 2006, the Texas Rangers picked him in the fifth
round, and he accepted the offer.

He experienced highs and lows in the big leagues. He was sent down to the minors in 2009, and it took a toll on his emotions.

His wife was a nurse in Dallas, and she worked twelve-hour shifts so she could make the long drive to watch him play.

"I told her I'm not going to keep doing this," he said. "It was back and forth from triple-A ball to the bigs, and I told her that if I didn't see a consistent future, I was going to stop playing and go back to college and get my degree and be a youth pastor."

By this time, he was twenty-four years old and had never really sought God's guidance in the decisions he made. But this is when his perspective began to change.

"I really, truly did not understand what it meant to walk with Jesus, even though I was brought up in church," he said. "I heard the terms but didn't know what it meant. I read my Bible here and there but wasn't consistent with it or my prayer life."

Chris started to dig into the Word of God. The more he dug, the more he discovered.

"I learned more about me, and I realized that baseball had a hold on me," he said. "I always knew it, but it became real to me. That is when I quit letting baseball run my life. I saw the big picture."

From that moment forward, Chris understood what it meant to have a personal relationship with Jesus Christ. He had missed the intimacy and need to be close to the Lord.

"I craved it," he said. "I had to be intentional about my relationship with God. I wanted it."

We love him, because he first loved us.

—1 John 4:19 KJV

What about you? Do you have the closeness with God you crave?

Has your job or other distractions formed a wedge between you and your walk with Christ? Are you just going through the motions?

On Deck

You might be in a similar situation where your job might have you coming and going with high demands and pressure. Perhaps you are on the road a lot and gone from your family more than you anticipated. You can do the work asked, but something is missing from your life. You always believed in God, but do you have that personal closeness He desires from you? Do you read His Word and pray every day? Or do you find yourself wandering out in right field?

Step Up to the Plate

The first thing you must realize is that these circumstances can happen to the best of people. Distractions can easily lead you away from the goodness God has to offer. One of the most endearing qualities about the Lord is His patience and His ability to forgive. But you have to recognize that you have drifted. You can still have a relationship with the Lord that is ordained by the Holy Spirit. It's your call to make it to the bullpen. Here are some warning signs to look for when you need to step up your relationship with God.

1. You stop praying. Satan is the only one who attempts to persuade you not to talk to God, and if you do this, your relationship will deteriorate. Imagine what would happen if you went four or five days without speaking to your spouse. This would definitely impact your intimacy, and her feelings would be hurt. God is also offended when we ignore Him. "If ye abide in me, and my words abide in you, ye shall ask what ye will, and it shall be done unto you" (John 15:7 KJV). Talk to the Lord . . . every day.

2. You stop reading the Bible. When you don't make reading God's word a priority, your heart becomes dead and cold. You must read the Word of God for daily strength and encouragement. If you don't eat food every day, your physical body begins to suffer. God uses the Bible to speak wisdom to you and to help you know His plans for you. Just like you need food to keep you strong and give you the energy you need to keep going, you need the Word. "As newborn babes, desire the sincere milk of the word, that ye may grow thereby" (1 Peter 2:2 KJV).

3. You quit going to church. Fellowship with your brothers and sisters in Christ is vital to your spiritual growth and success. If Chris quit showing up to work at the ball field, he would get kicked off the team. Employees do not keep their jobs if they only show up at the office whenever it is convenient for them. Your boss needs to depend on you to work hard and be dedicated. The same is true in your

Christian life. If you attend church regularly, even when you don't feel like going, you maintain your strength and are in good standing with the Savior and your church family. It's important to be on the field of play and be able to lean on the prayers of your fellow believers to hold you up in your grudge match against the devil.

4. You withdraw from people. Everyone needs encouragement and to be part of a team. The Orioles depend on Chris to hold down first base and play his role on the squad. When you stay away from your teammates—your family and friends—you lose the closeness needed for support. A wolf will prey on the one who has drifted from the fold. When you withdraw from your support and protection, you are an easy target. Stay close to your pack.

5. You feel lost and confused. The forces of evil want you off your game. They have the worst intentions for you, and they try to throw you off with doubts and fears. When this happens, stop what you are doing, sit down, take a deep breath, and speak the name of Jesus. Ask Him for clarification and to fill you with wisdom to know which path to choose. "For God is not the author of confusion, but of peace, as in all the churches of the saints" (1 Corinthians 14:33 KJV).

6. You rebel from what you know is right. Pride will lead you to feel superior to others and forget about where you came from. It will cause you to take your eye off the ball, and according to Proverbs 16:18,

pride will bring destruction. Be careful not to turn away from the truth and forget the fundamentals, or you will lose the game every time.

7. You listen to the lies of the devil. Satan is the master of untruths, and he wants you to abandon your faith. He will tell you that you are stupid and unworthy of God's love. He is a liar. When you hear the enemy whisper in your ear, remember this: "The Lord hath appeared of old unto me, saying, Yea, I have loved thee with an everlasting love: therefore with lovingkindness have I drawn thee" (Jeremiah 31:3 KJV).

8. You have the wrong motives. If you go to church, read your Bible, and serve others only because you feel obligated, then you need to reexamine yourself. While these things are good, your desires to do them should be genuine and all should be done out of your love for the Savior. Ask God to open doors for you to serve Him with your whole heart, and don't do any of these just to be seen by others.

"It took me eighteen years to really understand what it meant to have Christ be the center of my life," Chris said. "For some, it might take long and some not as long, but for me, that's what it took. I was sort of stubborn, but when I turned it all over to him, I was happy."

You too can have the joy and happiness that God wants you to have. Will you have problems? Yes. Will you be able to handle them better with the Lord at the helm? Definitely. Dig in and get closer to Christ. The sooner the better.

DAY 13

FIRST BIG-LEAGUE AT-BAT CHALLENGE

**Tony Graffanino:
Second Baseman,
Atlanta Braves**

By Scott McCausey

Humble yourselves, therefore, under the mighty hand of God so that at the proper time he may exalt you, casting all your anxieties on him, because he cares for you.
—1 Peter 5:6–7

Tony Graffanino found himself in the on-deck circle thousands of times, yet this trip was the dream of every Little Leaguer.

His head swiveled to find a blur of Braves fans cheering him on. His call to the big leagues that Friday evening in April wasn't expected, and neither was the fact his name was slotted number two on the lineup card. Earlier that day, he was assigned a locker and a uniform. He met teammates and future Hall of Famers Chipper Jones and John Smoltz, the starting pitcher of his first game.

The Crime Dog, Fred McGriff, was a few lockers down. He watched as his teammate, Marquis Grissom, stepped up to bat, and he murmured a prayer to tame the butterflies in his stomach. "Please God, allow Marquis to take his time at the plate. Help him be patient and wait for the right pitch."

His entire life was built for a time such as this. The countless pitches as a youngster in the backyard with his giant plastic bat, the travel games in Little League, Pony League, and high school—they all led to this moment.

The tools were at his disposal, and this gift was entrusted to him from above. But the stakes were never higher than this moment.

Tony studied the mound as the pitcher toed the rubber for the first throw of the ballgame.

This is Joey Hamilton, a veteran pitcher. I'm playing in the big leagues, he thought. The chest-high fastball was tapped too short, an easy play, and Marquis was retired for the first out for Atlanta. "So much for the long at-bat."

All our lives are filled with fearful, "first ever" moments. Regardless if it's the first time we drive a car, the first day on the job or at a new school, or our first opportunity to share Jesus with a stranger, our reliance on God has a big impact.

The apostle Paul learned on his journey to the big leagues that though he suffered from a thorn in his flesh, when he was weak, he was made strong through the power of Christ (2 Corinthians 12:7–10).

Our reliance on God should mimic this observation. Peter tells us we should take our worries, fears, and anxious thoughts to God, and even more importantly, we should do so with humility. When we confess our need for Christ's power, we give the glory to God.

Tony strode to the plate. His name was announced over the loudspeaker. But the only thing he heard was the pounding of his heart. As he dug at the front of the batter's box, his mind was spinning, and he struggled to simply breathe. "I've got to take the first pitch and settle in. If I can take a couple pitches, my stomach will relax, and I'll be able to concentrate."

Joey settled into his windup and delivered a fastball. It takes a ball four-tenths of a second if delivered at 95 mph to reach home plate. The ball has already traveled fifteen feet before the batter can gauge the basic direction it is traveling. As Tony attempted to absorb this first pitch experience, he received exactly what he bargained for. His reaction time was too slow, and the fastball struck him in the middle of his back as he turned to avoid being hit in the face.

He doesn't remember his reaction, and his recollection of how he made it to first is also a blur. As he reached base, the first-base coach patted his shoulder and said, "Did that hurt?" He saw his coach's lips move, but his pounding heart was still all he could hear.

"What?" he finally verbalized. The dazed look on his face painted a picture we all experience. "You just got hit in the back, did it hurt? Are you okay?" Tony's senses finally returned as the understanding of what just happened became real. His first official at-bat in the major league level was a hit by pitch.

God has a way of taking control of a situation. He got plunked, and it woke him up to the reality of his big-league dream. He finished the game getting his first big-league hit.

When pride comes, then comes disgrace,
but with humility comes wisdom.

—Proverbs 11:2 NIV

Taking lumps is never fun, and getting hit by a pitch can cause bruises, broken bones, or even serious injury. Tony took a fastball in the back during his first plate appearance in the majors, but he didn't spout or complain. He didn't charge the mound to accuse the pitcher of wrongdoing. He got up, dusted himself off, and trotted to first base to help advance his team to victory. We can follow that example just as Paul and the other champions in God's Word did. Will you be humble when you are challenged? Cast your cares on God, and understand He will protect you, guide you, and lift you up.

On Deck

In our weakness, God uses situations to get our attention and engage us in battle. It wakes us up to the reality of our calling, so our gifts are used to expand God's kingdom. Despite the fear of new beginnings and the understanding that a new start may prompt a trial we've never encountered, we don't face it alone. Paul reminds us how humble attitudes draw us close to Christ. He should know. He faced time alone in prison and persecution in the form of beatings far worse than a baseball to the back.

Step Up to the Plate

We all receive calls from God to accomplish big goals. We ready ourselves for new challenges through study of our current situation and an attitude of thanksgiving and excitement to Christ. Do you embrace the challenge you face? Tony was so nervous, he walked to the plate in a blur.

Your walk to the plate may also be difficult, but through reliance in Christ, the task can be conquered.

Here are some ways to embrace a challenge:

1. Embrace each opportunity for spiritual growth. No one has learned life lessons in times of joy and happiness.
2. You are human and not God. Challenges reveal limitations, and contrary to what you may have been taught, you don't know all the answers. A challenge will allow you to see the reality of your own weakness and cause you to depend on the Lord to knock in the game-winning run.
3. A challenge will invite humility. This is a blessing because it will make you depend on the Master in times of trouble. Jesus Himself embraced the challenge on the cross. If He had not done that, then you would not experience salvation.
4. A challenge is not about you. But it will lead you to examine your life and priorities. Even though God is big, He can become distant if you make your problems about you. Use them to praise Him and see where He wants to take you on your journey.

When you have the correct perspective, you can meet and overcome any obstacle or challenge thrown your way. The key is to send the Lord up to the plate so He can blast the pitch out of the park.

DAY 14
GOD WILL TAKE CARE OF YOU

Cody Allen:
Pitcher,
Los Angeles Angels of Anaheim

By Del Duduit

> And my God will meet all your needs according to the riches of his glory in Christ Jesus.
>
> —Philippians 4:19 NIV

"As long as you put your faith in the Lord, you will be taken care of no matter what happens," Cody Allen told me before a game in Cleveland. "That doesn't mean you won't ever have problems, but He will make sure you are okay."

The Angels relief pitcher grew up in a Christian home and regularly attended church with his family in Orlando, Florida. He said he loved the company of his brother, especially around the holidays.

He smiled and recalled one Christmas when he was a little boy and ran to the tree. He expected and anticipated several presents.

Instead, he found a note, which instructed him and his brother to go find a surprise. He and his brother followed the directions and dashed to the garage. He had no idea what awaited him. What could it be?

He flung open the door and discovered a fantastic and wonderful trampoline. "That was an awesome gift," he said. "I remember being excited, and we had so much fun on that thing."

However, he also said it led to a few broken arms and sprained wrists. "But it was fun," he added. "Such a cool gift." His parents took him to church and encouraged him to accept the gospel. He lived a fun and carefree childhood.

In eighth grade, Cody said he began to feel the Holy Spirit dealing with his heart. He didn't count on his upbringing to get him into heaven. He had to make his own decision. "It wasn't so much it was the right thing to do," he said. "I felt real conviction, and I wanted to live a life of integrity."

His life came to a crossroads. He knew his parents would still love him whether or not he made a commitment to live for Jesus. "I wanted to start living right because God wanted me to," he added. "It wasn't because I was raised in church. I was exposed to church, but I was the one who decided to live for the Lord."

Has Cody lived a problem-free life? No.

He is a regular guy with normal problems like everyone else. But he does not consume himself with troubles, and he appreciates the joy he has in his life. Worry has become a distant part of his past. "God is not going to turn his head and just let us go off and die," he said. "He has told me that He will take care of me, and I trust Him."

He often reflects on stories from the Bible when he is confronted with a problem in life. One of his favorites is the story of when Moses led the children of Israel out of Egypt. By faith, Moses confronted Pharaoh with boldness in the name of the Lord and guided God's chosen people out of bondage. Moses did not fear because he knew the Holy Spirit provided shelter and protection.

He trusted in the Lord and took a stand. "I love the Exodus series in the Bible," Cody said. "I think a lot of people constantly worry about circumstance, and they worry about not being taken care of."

Cody leans on the Lord for his everyday needs, yet he does not let them become a distraction. He has a high-pressure, high-profile job and is aware he must perform when his coaches summon him to the game. Professional baseball is a game of failure.

If a batter posts an average of .300, he is considered a reliable hitter. It means he will get a hit in three out of ten plate appearances—which also means he makes seven outs. A hitter will fail more times than succeed. "Every night I am not going to have my best stuff on the mound," he said. "But there are games when I do. The same is true in life—there are bad weeks and good ones. But I'll take a bad week with the Lord any time, because I know it's going to be okay in the end." He knows he will have joyous times and difficult ones.

There will be occasions when Cody gives up a game-winning home run, and there will be times when he strikes out the side. He takes it in stride and is confident the Lord will always be there for him. This keeps him going.

I can do all this through him who gives me strength.
—Philippians 4:13 NIV

On Deck

Are you worried about a current situation? You are not alone. Worry and fear are natural human emotions. But if you do it too often, your health may be impacted. Chronic worrying can affect your daily life, and it can interfere with your appetite, lifestyle habits, sleep, relationships, and performance on the job or at school. This burden can lead to anxiety, depression, and harsh habits like cigarettes, alcohol, and drug use. If you are in this place in life, you have a decision to make. Would you rather continue to fret and suffer these harmful results, or will you give your problems over to the Lord for Him to handle? Which do you think will lead to the most happiness?

Step Up to the Plate

You made the right choice and gave your troubles over to the Lord. Now what? Is it normal to harbor doubt in your heart? Maybe. But here are some scripture passages you can look to for reassurance.

1. "Cast your cares on the Lord, / and he will sustain you; / he will never let / the righteous be shaken" (Psalm 55:22 NIV). The Lord wants your burdens. He will bear them for you so you can enjoy life and praise Him.
2. "Who of you by worrying can add a single hour to your life?" (Luke 12:25 NIV). Worrying does not accomplish one thing or improve your situation.

If you stew and fuss over something you cannot control, you are only wasting valuable time.

3. "For God has not given us a spirit of fear, but of power and of love and of a sound mind" (2 Timothy 1:7 NKJV). The devil tries to make you afraid so you will surrender. This verse means to seek God in prayer and find the strength to continue.

4. "I lift up my eyes to mountains— / where does my help come from? / My help comes from the Lord, / the Maker of heaven and earth. / He will not let your foot slip— / he who watches over you will not slumber" (Psalm 121:1–3 NIV). If you are a parent and have ever watched your child sleep, you can relate. Just know, you are God's child, and He will protect you at all times.

5. "Indeed, the very hairs of your head are all numbered" (Luke 12:7 NIV). This incredible verse shows you how important you are in the eyes of the Lord. When you are discouraged, trust in God and believe He knows everything about you and claims you as His own.

You will enjoy happiness when you cast your burdens on the Lord. But when you experience times of doubt and fear, reflect on these verses for strength and reassurance. Do a search for others, as there are many more passages throughout the Bible that provide comfort and inspiration. Or you can do what Cody does and read the Exodus series of miracles. If the Lord can talk to Moses through a burning bush, imagine the incredible and spectacular ways He can reveal Himself to you.

DAY 15
WHY GET INVOLVED?

Tim Tebow:
Outfielder,
New York Mets

By Del Duduit

And though I have the gift of prophecy, and understanding all mysteries, and all knowledge; and though I have all faith, so that I could remove mountains, and have not charity, I am nothing.

—1 Corinthians 13:2 KJV

Tim Tebow started his foundation to help a population in need. His parents were missionaries in the Philippines, and he had seen firsthand how much it means to people when you show them love, compassion, and Christ.

The sole purpose of the Tim Tebow Foundation is to bring faith, hope, and love to those needing a brighter day in their darkest hour.

Several ministries operate under the umbrella, such as the Night to Shine Prom, Orphan Care, and Adoption Aid to name a few.

Tim has been instrumental in opening hospitals through his charitable foundation, and he does this because he has a love for people through his relationship with Christ.

He has been blessed with resources through his abilities and talents, and he obeys God's commandment to give back.

Tim does not give to others for attention. He gives because he serves a Savior who gave him salvation.

"God's love is amazing, and we are called to be a light and give back," he said.

My wife and I volunteer at his Night to Shine Prom event each year in Huntington, West Virginia. We both give our time and shine shoes for those attending the prom. When we see the looks on the faces of these special needs people, we are so blessed. Just a few hours of service can make a person's entire week (or longer) and cause them to smile and feel important.

"It's going to affect you just as much as you are going to affect them," Tim said. "It's amazing in God's economy when we go and serve, that we are more fulfilled than we would be by doing anything else."

He went on to say that serving doesn't always make sense to the world, and that many people don't understand why Christians want to help.

"We show love to people that a lot of the world hasn't loved," he said. "And it does something to us, and that's why it's my favorite night of the year. It's hundreds of thousands of people coming together to celebrate God's love for humanity—for everyone—not just some—but all. Because we are all worthy and we all have identity that God gave us, and we are all unique and special."

> And now abideth faith, hope, charity, these three; but the
> greatest of these is charity.
>
> —1 Corinthians 13:13 KJV

Do you give back? Have you volunteered to help those less
fortunate than you? Will you serve others with a thankful
heart?

On Deck

Have you ever passed up the opportunity to participate
with a charitable organization? I encourage you to humble
yourself and make room in your life for at least one that is
important to you. You will be taken out of your comfort
zone when you help those in need, but it is a great learning
experience and will make you so thankful for all God has
given you.

Step Up to the Plate

Maybe you don't have the resources and celebrity status
that Tim has to help draw worldwide attention to a cause.
But there are many ways you can help. Check out the
suggestions below on how to get involved and make a
difference.

1. Research your charity and organization. There are
   thousands of organizations that have intentions
   of helping those who are less fortunate, but sadly
   not all are honest. Take time to conduct research
   or reach out to people you know who might be

involved with charitable or civic groups to try to find the best one for you to embrace and support.

2. Pray about becoming involved. Once you find the charity that pulls on your heart strings, pray and ask God to open the doors for you to explore getting involved and helping. Send an email or make a call and get the ball rolling.

3. Stay involved. Don't be a one-timer. If the group meets quarterly, put the meeting dates on your calendar. Go all-in and show up on a regular basis. Dedicate yourself to become a dependable team player to help make the organization successful. Tim said you will be more fulfilled by giving back to others, and he's right.

4. Hold a fundraiser. Contribute by organizing a way to help the organization financially. Most are nonprofit groups and need funds to operate. Chip in with your time and money.

5. Inspire others to get involved. Once you are in deep and blessed for taking part, talk the charity up to your friends and encourage them to help out through word of mouth and social media. The Night to Shine Prom started out with forty-four churches involved, and in 2019, there were 655 churches that hosted events.

6. Give what you can. Maybe you can't spare a lot of money to support the group. That's okay. Give what you can from the heart and include the group in your prayers. You can make a difference with

your time, and perhaps you can budget a few dollars each week.

7. Volunteer at a soup kitchen or homeless shelter. You can find these in any major city or surrounding towns. Homelessness is a huge problem in our country, and there is also a need for food and clothing. Take time each month to go, serve, and converse. Many of the people who go there have amazing stories and just need to talk with and pray with someone. You could be that person.

8. Take a mission trip. Research the various missionary organizations and pray for God to point you to the right one. Save up your money and look for sponsors to help you travel overseas to work in the mission field for a couple of weeks.

9. Donate unwanted items. Go through your home and find items and clothing you don't use anymore. Make sure the items are still in good shape and usable. You might even buy some new clothing or donate a gift card to help people pick out their own wardrobe. Buy some nonperishable and personal hygiene items to have on hand when you find out about someone in need.

When you reach out to help other people, you will be blessed by God. You might not be able to solve all the problems in the world, but you can take time to focus on being a blessing to a small group. Make someone smile. You can show Christ to them, and that's worth more than all the gold in the world.

DAY 16
LIFE CAN BE A WALK IN THE BALLPARK

Curtis Granderson:
All-Star Outfielder,
Miami Marlins

By Del Duduit

For I long to see you, that I may impart to you some spiritual gift to strengthen you—that is, that we may be mutually encouraged by each other's faith, both yours and mine.

—Romans 1:11–12

No one has a problem-free life. Not even Curtis Granderson.

But you would never know it by talking to him.

The three-time MLB All-Star won the Silver Slugger Award in 2011 and the prestigious Roberto Clemente Award in 2016.

He's been named the Marvin Miller Man of the Year four times throughout his career, and he was the American League RBI leader in 2011.

Many fans entertain the idea that professional athletes don't have problems like anyone else. They are well paid, drive fancy cars, and live in big mansions.

But even successful athletes have problems.

"Life has not been a walk in the park," he said. "We all have struggles and challenges. There is always a lot of stuff going on."

Professional baseball players have issues to deal with like other people.

"There is a role model/fandom/stardom that people have of us, and they think we are all supermen," Curtis added. "They think nothing affects us—that we don't get sick, or we don't get hurt, or that we don't have family issues. None of that happens to us they think."

But in real life, MLB players experience heartache and encounter everyday obstacles that we all face.

"I was just talking to a couple of buddies of mine that I grew up with and who I've known since the first grade," he recalled. "We all have stuff going on, and we always like to check in with each other and see how we are doing. The usual 'how are your parents?' or 'how are the kids?' Stuff like that."

His buddies help to keep him grounded, and they lean on one another for advice.

"We enjoy talking about our lives—the good and the bad," he added. "It's all about having a combination of people that God has blessed you with in your lives, so at times you can communicate and just vent, or you can just listen."

The best part about having friends is you can let them know they are not alone during a time of trial.

"We all need people like this," Curtis said. "Especially in this game—we all need each other because we are gone a lot from our family."

Having a support system of people outside of the diamond is special for Curtis. "I stay in contact with some friends who knew me before I played baseball, and we help each other. It's been worth it to have some great friends. They will call or text and just reach out and check in and that's special."

Throughout his star-studded career, Curtis has experienced the highs and the lows.

"But you know, through it all, I've got some wonderful friends who have helped me through the good and bad times," he said. "Without them, and without God, I'd be lost."

> And this commandment we have from him: whoever loves God must also love his brother.
>
> —1 John 4:21

Are you there for your brother in Christ in the good times and bad? Do you make the effort to reach out to your friends and encourage them?

On Deck

Being a successful player in professional baseball has its rewards, including recognition, fame, and money. Curtis has learned to accept his stardom, but he also knows he's put on a pedestal that is unrealistic. Baseball players go through times of struggle just like you. And due to their fame, their problems often become public and they don't get the chance to deal with them in private. You also may encounter challenging circumstances. Maybe you receive disturbing health news from your doctor or you find out your company wants to transfer you across the country. Do you have a support system in place to help with unexpected adjustments? Do you reach out and check in on your friends to see how they are coping with life?

Step Up to the Plate

True friends are hard to come by. If you are blessed with some, thank the Lord for them. You can set the example and be the supportive person you want to be to them. Hopefully, they will reciprocate and be there for you too. You don't have to wait for a family tragedy to reach out. A simple text message or a quick email to let them know you are praying for them does not take long. Here are some characteristics of being a genuine and sincere friend.

1. You will show respect. Honor your true friends and make them feel valuable and loved. Try to see your friends through the eyes of Christ and be there for them in times of trouble with a listening ear. "Whoever belittles his neighbor lacks sense, / but a man of understanding remains silent" (Proverbs 11:12).

2. You will forgive. We all make mistakes and often need forgiveness. Cut your friends some slack when they mess up and be there to support them and help pick up the pieces. When you can show kindness and love, you are a friend.

3. You will support. When you go through a struggle, you will discover who your true friends really are.

Anyone can be there during celebrations and give you high fives. But the friends who come around when you're feeling down and need lifting up are your real friends. They will listen to you and pray with you and are not afraid to tell you when you do something you shouldn't.

4. You will hold them accountable. True friends will let you know when you are making the wrong choices. They might encourage you to hold off on making a phone call to someone you are upset with and get you to calm down and reconsider. Or they may suggest you don't go to certain places for fear it might damage your reputation. A true friend will hold you to high godly standards. "Iron sharpens iron, and one man sharpens another" (Proverbs 27:17).

5. Set boundaries. Never let someone take advantage of your friendship. You must establish rules and expectations to ensure you are protected. Your true friends will never put you in a compromising position. "Let your foot be seldom in your neighbor's house, / lest he have his fill of you and hate you" (Proverbs 25:17).

Life will not be a walk in the park, as Curtis said. But when you have true friends, they make the journey around the bases more enjoyable and fun. Be the best friend you can be. And always remember that Jesus is a friend who sticks closer than any brother.

DAY 17
APPRECIATE THE SMALL THINGS

Daniel Norris:
Pitcher,
Detroit Tigers

By Del Duduit

There is nothing better for a man, than that he should eat and drink, and that he should make his soul enjoy good in his labour. This also I saw, that it was from the hand of God.

—Ecclesiastes 2:24 KJV

The simple things in life are the best.

There is nothing better than a cool glass of lemonade on a hot day or sitting with your children and eating hot dogs at a baseball game.

Simple things.

Sometimes people can complicate life with objects they don't need. They might buy them just because they can, or they might go into debt to keep up with the neighbors.

Daniel Norris is not like that. He is a pitcher in the MLB and makes a nice living for his family. But that's not where he places his worth.

"More than anything, I just know that I play for the Lord in all that I do," he said, "It's not like something that is turned off when you're not on the field. It's living for Christ in all things."

He's never been interested in living the lavish lifestyle some professional athletes live. He said if that's what they want to do, that's fine, but it's not him.

"I try to surround myself with simple things in life like the mountains and nature," he said. "That's what I enjoy. I'm inspired by it, and it's how I grew up."

His family owned a bicycle shop in Johnson City, Tennessee, for nearly a century. There he was taught the values he still embraces today. To be honest, Daniel would much rather drive his 1978 van than a fancy car. And he still serves the Lord with all his heart.

"He is why I am where I am today," he said. "That's why I am able to be a good father at home and continue to be a good husband and a good player. God has provided all that for me . . . and I'm grateful."

His humble beginnings and service to the Lord have made him appreciate the simple things in life. He describes himself as a conservative minimalist who doesn't need a lot to be happy.

"I love God's handiwork and what He has created," he said. "I can hike, ski, surf, camp, do lots of things. I want to share that with everyone so they can experience God's handiwork too."

He is grateful he can earn a nice living for his family, but he doesn't see the need for all of it.

"Who am I to deserve that? What have I really done?" He said. "I'm actually more comfortable being kind of poor."

Daniel said he will always resist conformity and enjoys his "simple" lifestyle.

"As long as I have the Lord and my family, then I'm happy," he said.

> Charge them that are rich in this world, that they be not highminded, nor trust in uncertain riches, but in the living God, who giveth us richly all things to enjoy.
> —1 Timothy 6:17 KJV

Do you need more "things" in your life to be happy? Is God's love not enough?

On Deck

Society has placed an emphasis on celebrity and owning the nicest things in life money can buy. It's easy to be awarded credit and encouraged to go into debt. People are fascinated with movie stars and will go to extremes to live a life of luxury. Are you this way? Do you have to have the latest iPhone even though you might not be able to afford the price? Do you give in to the temptations to go on a shopping spree because you can? Do you feel you must have the latest fashions? Do you try to impress your neighbors with fancy and electronic gadgets?

Step Up to the Plate

There is nothing wrong with having nice things. But when they take priority over what God has for you, there is a problem. You should never go too far into debt to stay up with the trends. Your credit rating could be impacted, and your obligations could cost you more in the long run than you anticipated. You need to live within your means, and you don't have to travel the world to have a wonderful life. If you can afford the price tag that's wonderful, and I say to go for it and have fun. But there are many ways to enjoy life—a simple life—as a believer. You don't have to be rich and famous to have fun. Being a Christian is the best lifestyle anyone could ever want or hope for. Here are some reasons why serving the Lord is worth it in the long run.

1. Your debt of sin is forgiven. This fact is worth more than all the gold in the world. To have your sins tossed into the sea of God's forgetfulness is a miracle. This should put a spring in your step and a song in your heart. Or in Daniel's case, some zip on his fastball. "If we confess our sins, he is faithful and just to forgive us our sins, and to cleanse us from all unrighteousness" (1 John 1:9 KJV).

2. You are set free from the bondage of sin. There is no price to put on the freedom the Lord gives you. When you are a Christian, you no longer have the weight of sin on your shoulders.

3. You have peace and joy. The happiness the Master grants you is worth more than any multiyear contract you might sign.

4. Your every need is supplied. When the Lord is your coach, you don't have to worry about your needs. He will supply them. Now, keep in mind, Christ

will give you what you *need*, not necessarily what you *want*. There is a big difference.

5. You have a mansion waiting on you in heaven. God promised to prepare a place for you, and that's what you will receive. Just imagine, a mansion in heaven awaits you. When this life is over, it won't matter where you lived on earth or what your income bracket was. The most important thing is where you will spend eternity. "In my Father's house are many mansions: if it were not so, I would have told you. I go to prepare a place for you" (John 14:2 KJV).

Baseball is Daniel's passion. He loves the competition and is blessed to play at a high level. But this does not keep him from enjoying the simple things in life. He would much rather drive an older car, hike through the mountains of Tennessee, and pray with his children than have all the riches this world can offer.

DAY 18
DO YOU HEAR WHAT HE SAYS?

Dave Jauss:
Coach and Scout,
New York Yankees

By Del Duduit

So, faith comes from hearing, and hearing through the word of Christ.

—Romans 10:17

Before Dave broke into coaching in the MLB, he grew up in a Christian home in Chicago.

He went to church and Sunday school and was involved in the youth group.

He grew up in a generation that possessed a spirit about them to do good for everyone—their teachers, parents, and coaches.

Dave was no exception.

"I thought I could do some good, and I did," he said. "I was good in school and well behaved. I was a good athlete, and then later had a good opportunity to coach at the professional level."

He was a successful coach, and he had a good wife and children. "I thought I was better than the guy next to me because I could control things . . . at least I thought," Dave said.

The years went by and his wife, Billie, made him see that he was putting his career ahead of everything else in their lives—including their marriage.

Why don't I just fix it? Dave thought. But he couldn't.

The couple cared enough about each other to make it work, so they found their way to a non-Christian marriage counselor who advised them to go to church together.

They took the advice, went to church, found the Lord, and placed their marriage in the center of His will. They grew closer and experienced true happiness that only God can provide.

"I realized that I had been deaf to what God had been asking me all along," he said. "I thought I had served Him my whole life, but I didn't honestly hear Jesus preached from the pulpit growing up as a kid."

As his relationship with God grew stronger, Dave was able to release the control he wanted to have over his own life.

"I gave my life to Him—I really turned it over to the Lord," he said. "At that moment, things were right. I was full, and He made me appreciate my family and my baseball career more."

As a coach, Dave tries to help the younger players coming up in the big leagues and wants to be an encouragement. He does not push his salvation experience on anyone, but he makes sure his life reflects the Bible to players who have never experienced Christ.

"If they have any questions for me, I tell them the story about how God changed my life," he said. "I make sure they hear me and know what happened."

Do not be conformed to this world, but be transformed by
the renewal of your mind, that by testing you may discern
what is the will of God, what is good and acceptable and
perfect.

—Romans 12:2

Do you listen to God?

On Deck

Your life might be like Dave's. You may have a good job,
a good wife, and beautiful children, but you have no
happiness and satisfaction. You might all go to church
together and appear to everyone to have the perfect life.
You might drive a new car every two years and take dream
vacations that make your friends envious. There is nothing
wrong with having these possessions, but when they take
priority over the Lord and come before your family, you are
asking for problems. In today's hustle and bustle society,
you can lose focus of what is important. You can have a
fantastic job and possessions, but these things can lose their
luster and appeal over time. They can become bigger than
your life and dictate your time and attention.

Step Up to the Plate

Dave was blessed to have a wife who recognized they had
a problem and did something about it. She wanted her
marriage to work. If you find yourself in a similar situation
to Dave, then take action and do something about it. You
cannot hear the words of the Lord if you are far from His

presence. God may be speaking to you, but you are distant because of the things of the world. Here are some ways to get closer to the Lord and "hear" what He says to you.

1. Spend quiet time alone with God. If you lack His presence, try turning off the distractions such as your cell phone or the computer. Take a walk or find a quiet spot to talk with God. Your spouse feels appreciated when you plan a date night just for her. Think how God feels if you give Him a few minutes of your day to thank Him for all His blessings. Grow your connection with the Head Coach, and you will find that your relationships with those closest to you will become stronger.

2. Increase your time reading His word. Underline some of your favorite passages, memorize inspirational verses, and take notes. When you dive deeper in studying the Bible, your loved ones will see more of Christ in you. "All scripture is breathed out by God and profitable for teaching, for reproof, for correction, and for training in righteousness" (2 Timothy 3:16).

3. Journal your thoughts. Jot down your thoughts and put on paper how good God has been to you each day. Take time over the next few days to review these and remind yourself of God's goodness.

4. Appreciate His creation. When you look at a sunset or the moon, marvel at His imagination. When you can appreciate His wonderful design in nature and you, then you can appreciate His masterful plan

to give you eternal life. "Therefore, since we have been justified by faith, we have peace with God through our Lord Jesus Christ" (Romans 5:1).

Dave's wife brought their situation to his attention, and they both heard from God. Dave never knew the kind of relationship he could have with the Lord until he listened. Seek the plan of Christ, and He will tell you when to round third and head for home to win the game.

DAY 19

HIS NAME IS WRITTEN DOWN

Al Oliver:
Batting Champion,
World Series Champion,
Pittsburgh Pirates

By Del Duduit

Jesus answered him, "Truly, truly, I say to you, unless one
is born again he cannot see the kingdom of God."

—John 3:3

On paper, there is no doubt that Al Oliver should be in the
Baseball Hall of Fame in Cooperstown, New York.

He was selected to seven All-Star teams, was a vital
part of the 1971 World Series with the Pittsburgh Pirates,
and won three Silver Slugger Awards. In 1982, he was the
National League Batting Champion and led the league in
RBIs.

But when his name first appeared on the ballot for
sportswriters to consider him for induction into the Hall of
Fame, he came up short.

Al did not receive enough votes to be put back on the
ballot the next go around.

In 2019, his name was presented to the Modern Era
Committee for consideration into the prestigious Hall of
Fame. This committee addresses players who might have

been left off the ballot for unusual reasons and may have been overlooked due to outstanding circumstances.

The small group of ten said no. As a result, he will never be inducted into baseball's elite group.

His stats are more impressive than many who are already in the Hall of Fame.

"It's out of my control," Al said to me over coffee one day in his hometown of Portsmouth, Ohio. "It's not up to me. The only thing I could have done is play ball—and I did that pretty well."

Everywhere Al goes, the Hall of Fame is brought up to him.

He always has an honest but canned response.

"I thank them for their comments because they respect my career," he noted.

Pete Rose told me once that Al was the best line drive hitter he had ever seen.

Jim Palmer told me that Al was special because he could "hit my best pitches."

Is Al disappointed to know that his name will not be enshrined where it—by all rights—should be written?

"It's just something that I have to deal with and accept," he said. "I definitely did my best as a player under some tough situations."

Even in his late thirties, when most players are out of the game, Al still played and produced.

"That's the way I was brought up," he said. "You play hard, you give it your best, and you trust God with the rest."

Al has every right to be bitter and disappointed. But he's not.

"There is always something to deal with," he said. "I lost my parents at a young age and had to deal with that. God was in control then, and He's in control now. I'm not angry because I did my best, and it's just part of life. It's gratifying to know that so many people think I should be in the Hall of Fame, and that's all that matters."

Al also said that his main goal is to reach Heaven's Hall of Fame.

"I know I'll be there," he added with a chuckle.

Jesus said to him, "I am the way, and the truth, and the life. No one comes to the Father except through me."
—John 14:6

Is making heaven your ambition?

On Deck

Perhaps you live a good life. You give to the poor and go to church when you can. You sing in the choir and even tithe your money. You obey the golden rule and help out your neighbor and friends. You work hard and never talk bad about anyone. You even donate your time to charity and serve as a mentor to local youth. But is that enough to get you into heaven? Or perhaps your life is just the opposite. You have not lived up to your potential and have disappointed those around you. Can you still find your way to heaven?

Step Up to the Plate

All the good things you have done in your life are important, and they matter. The world needs kind and loving people in every community. But works by themselves will not allow you entry into God's Hall of Fame. You must ask Jesus into your heart, and here's how.

1. See your need of Christ. No matter your circumstances in life, you need to be saved. Recognize you are a sinner and stand in need of a Savior. Whether you have lived a productive life or one that has been less than fulfilling, you need the Lord. "There is therefore now no condemnation for those who are in Christ Jesus" (Romans 8:1).

2. Believe. In your heart, you must know that Jesus was born of a virgin, lived a sinless life, died for your sins, and arose three days later to defeat death, hell, and the grave.

3. Ask for forgiveness. "If we confess our sins, he is faithful and just to forgive us our sins and to cleanse us from all unrighteousness" (1 John 1:9).

4. Accept the gift of salvation. God has gone to prepare a place for you in heaven. Make plans to go. "In my Father's house are many rooms. If it were not so, would I have told you that I go to prepare a place for you?" (John 14:2).

5. Live and be an ambassador for Him. Read you Bible every day, pray daily, and attend a church on

a regular basis. Don't judge others, and do what's right in the eyes of God.

Al will never find his way into the halls of Cooperstown, New York. Does he deserve to have his name listed there with those who are considered baseball's immortals? Many experts believe he does, but this is not going to happen. Al says it's more important for his kids and grandkids to know that he will make heaven his home one day. "That's the best legacy I can leave them," he added.

DAY 20
WHY ARE YOU HERE?

Adam Cimber:
Pitcher,
Cleveland Indians

By Del Duduit

Now you are the body of Christ, and members individually.
—1 Corinthians 12:27 NKJV

There is a lot of press associated with being a professional baseball player. One day you can be the star of the team, and the next day you might face an onslaught of boos from your fans.

A big hitter might blast a game-winning home run on Monday night then strike out four times on Tuesday.

You are only as good as your last outing.

Adam Cimber, pitcher for the Cleveland Indians, knows all about the everyday demands he encounters.

The Portland, Oregon, native must take care of his body and spend time in the weight room. He has to stay in tip-top condition and make sure he eats the right food to remain healthy. There are times when he must face the media and be an ambassador for his organization.

He also must pay attention to fans and maintain a positive image within the community. And, oh yes, let's not forget he must go out in front of thousands of people and pitch to the best of his ability.

But Adam, who was raised in a Christian home and in a solid church, was taught his real worth as a person.

He knows at the end of the day that what he does to glorify God is all that matters.

"That is what everything is all about," he said. "When I come out here and feel the stress of baseball, what always brings me to the center and where I need to be as a person is realizing why I am here on earth."

Adam likes to let others know what he stands for. The first word on his Twitter profile lists him as a Christian and then a baseball player.

"Sometimes it's easy to get wrapped up in who I am in the eyes of fans and the things of this world," he added. "But when you step back and come back to God, He always puts life in perspective. Nothing matters except how you treat others and how you love the Lord and how you serve others as a believer."

In 2017, Adam was left back in extended spring training with the San Diego Padres. At the time, he entertained thoughts that his baseball career might be in jeopardy and didn't respond the way he should have to the potential bad news.

"I thought to myself that if I could not play baseball, then who would I become?" he said. "If I'm not a baseball player—who am I?"

Adam soon reflected back on how he was raised, and he realized his relationship with God was not where it needed to be for him to handle this situation.

"I realized through all of those tough times where I needed to put my identity," he said. "I had to make God the center of my life, and everything else would fall into place and that if I was to pitch, then that would be icing on the cake."

He listened to his heart and made a stronger commitment to be the Christian example he needed to be.

"That is when I started to have a more in-depth and personal relationship with Jesus," he admitted. "I started praying more and reading my Bible more. I felt like I was in an actual relationship with God again instead of going through the motions."

Adam rediscovered his real identity, and it was not his role as a professional pitcher. He enjoys being a member of the Indians, but he knows his responsibility as a child of God is on a higher playing field.

> For we are His workmanship, created in Christ Jesus for good works, which God prepared beforehand that we should walk in them.
>
> —Ephesians 2:10 NKJV

Who are you?

On Deck

Do you place your identity in your line of work? Perhaps you live in the past and look back on days in the past when you were more successful than you are today in the eyes of the world. Maybe you have an important role in life and feel that you are more valuable than others whom you associate with. Has your ego become inflated to the point that you place yourself higher than others around you? This can happen so easily, especially when you have obligations to meet and people depend on you for success. Or maybe your life is the opposite, and you struggle with finding your identity. Perhaps you feel lost and invisible to others around you and long for others to notice who you are and the talents you possess.

Step Up to the Plate

Don't let your occupation in life dominate who you are as a person. Adam fulfills his obligations as a pitcher and does it well. But he also uses his platform to honor God. Here are some ways you can reclaim your identity in Christ, no matter what your occupation might be.

1. Family is first. Your loved ones should be your top priority. If your boss needs you to work late and prepare a presentation when your son has a game, then find a way to get the job done after your son's event. If your daughter has an evening band concert, do your best to be there. And if your wife wants you to go out to dinner on a date, put the work and the phone on hold. There are times when your job needs to come first, but it should never be your top priority.

2. Give of your time. Make it a point to volunteer at a charity of your choice on a regular basis. Become involved with a nonprofit organization and stay faithful. When you give your time for a worthy

cause, you will be blessed as much as those whose lives you touch.

3. Give your money. God commands you to give a portion of what you earn to Him. After all, He provided you with the job to make the income and giving back to God is a way of praising Him for his many blessings on you and your family. Don't give Him your leftovers. "Honor the Lord with your possessions, / and with the firstfruits of all your increase" (Proverbs 3:9 NKJV).

4. Find ways to minister. There are simple ways to inspire others such as posting verses on your social media profile, like Adam does. You don't have to be a minister in order to have a ministry. Consider making regular visits to the local hospital or taking food to nurses on the late shift at a hospice facility. There are many ways you can have an impact for God.

Adam had to face a trial to realize his need to be a child of God. If you're not sure what God wants for your life, ask Him to help you find your identity through Him. Adam is known to many as a pitcher, but he knows he is much more than that in the eyes of the Master. Christ has a plan for you, but you must trust Him to put you in the game at the right time. You are important to Him. This is who you are—and don't ever forget that.

DAY 21
BREAK THE SLUMP

Chris Davis:
All-Star First Baseman,
Baltimore Orioles

By Del Duduit

Therefore we do not lose heart. Though outwardly we are wasting away, yet inwardly we are being renewed day by day. For our light and momentary troubles are achieving for us an eternal glory that far outweighs them all. So we fix our eyes not on what is seen, but on what is unseen, since what is seen is temporary, but what is unseen is eternal.

—2 Corinthians 4:16–18 NIV

Fifty-four plate appearances without a hit.

That's what Chris Davis dealt with in 2019.

On April 13, he smacked a line drive single that scored two runs against the Boston Red Sox to snap the skid. When the day ended, he added two more doubles on the day.

The monkey was off his back.

Relief. Satisfaction.

Chris endured a long slump that dated back to the end of the 2018 season.

Fans were getting frustrated with Chris's lack of productivity at the plate, and the media were relentless. He faced questions every day from reporters, and his mind began to play games with him. He thought about it all the time because he had never gone through something this long and difficult.

The drought was uncharted waters for a player who was accustomed to producing at the plate. In 2013, he was selected to the MLB All-Star Team. The same year, he won the Silver Slugger Award, and he led the league in home runs in 2013 and 2015.

But Chris kept working to build up his confidence in the batter's box. He studied films of pitchers and tried not to let the situation distract him.

He finally had to give it over to God and let Him swing the bat.

"I had to remind myself that He is always there for you, even when you go through trials," Chris said. "You might not feel like it at times, but He cares about you and is thinking about you all the time. He cares so deeply for you and me that He sent His son to die for us."

This was the perspective Chris needed to maintain. After all, he was just trying to hit a baseball. But this is his occupation, and he wasn't performing well.

"No matter what happens, if you are a success at your job or not, God loves you the same if I'm in a slump or not—day in and day out."

Chris battled with his identity in baseball and concluded that if he went 0-5 at the plate or 3-4 Christ loved him regardless.

"You just keep swinging," Chris added. "You surround yourself with good people who will speak the truth to you, who will support you, and who will pray for you."

> When the righteous cry for help, the Lord hears
> and delivers them out of all their troubles.
> The Lord is near to the brokenhearted
> and saves the crushed in spirit.
>
> —Psalm 34:17–18

The same applies to you if you are in a spiritual slump. Have you ever felt your prayers are falling on deaf ears? Have you ever wanted to give up on your journey of faith?

On Deck

Has something happened in your life that has caused you to fall into a spiritual depression? Perhaps someone close to you has let you down by breaking your trust. Maybe you lost your job in a layoff, you have experienced health issues, or you have a special prayer that has gone unanswered for a number of years and your faith is wavering.

Step Up to the Plate

All these scenarios are real and can impact you spiritually if you let your guard down. The pressures and demands of life can cause you to want to hide from society. Maybe you feel that God has forgotten you. Just know that He has placed you on a journey that is uniquely yours. Satan will try to bring you down and make you feel there is no way to get back on top. But you can take some obvious steps when you find yourself at the plate and the bat feels like it weighs thirty-five pounds.

1. Pray. Find a place each day to commune with God. Turn all your problems over to Him and get out of the way. "Then you will call upon me and come and pray to me, and I will hear you" (Jeremiah 29:12).

2. Get more involved. To get your mind off temporary problems, look for some positive distractions. Get more active in your church, volunteer at a homeless shelter, or look for a conference or retreat that might provide you with the encouragement you need. "Whoever is generous to the poor lends to the Lord, / and he will repay him for his deed" (Proverbs 19:17).

3. Take a break. Go on a vacation and unwind. If you can't afford one or don't have time to take from work, then unplug on the weekend and get away for a brief time to unwind and get some rest. You can't run away from your problems, but you might be able to get your mind off of them for a little while.

4. Talk it out. Find a mentor, a pastor, or a close friend and meet them for coffee. Make sure you pick someone you can confide in who will speak life into your situation. Tell them what you are going through and listen to their advice. Find comfort and security in fellowship. "Bear one another's

burdens, and so fulfill the law of Christ" (Galatians 6:2).

5. Do something different. Join a gym or find a hobby you enjoy and spend more time in that area. Break up your routine. At times, hitters might switch batting gloves or wear different socks to a game if they are in a slump. Change things up and find a new approach to the day.

Chris went through a fifty-four-at-bat slump that wore on his thoughts and mind. He remained frustrated until he let it go and let God go to bat for him. Once you recognize you are going through a valley, know that through it all He loves you and will be there to high-five you when you smack the line drive up the middle. Endure, keep the faith, and trust in Jesus.

DAY 22
LET YOUR VOICE BE HEARD

Daniel Stumpf:
Pitcher,
Detroit Tigers

By Del Duduit

Let the field exult, and everything in it!
Then shall all the trees of the forest sing for joy.
—Psalm 96:12

You will always see two things on Daniel Stumpf's baseball gloves and gear when he takes the diamond: Psalm 96:12 and the name of his son.

For Daniel, it's the perfect way for everyone to see what's important to him.

He was born and raised in church in Humble, Texas, and his brother is a pastor.

"It [church] was all we knew growing up," he said. "We went to worship all the time. We didn't think about it because it was what we did."

When he made it to the MLB, he knew he would have a lot of eyes on him.

That's why he chose to put scripture on his gloves and anything else that is visible.

"It's the perfect voice for me," he said. "When people see my glove, they know that God and my faith are a big part of my life."

Daniel does his best to maintain and keep a strong and positive reputation on and off the field, but he admits he is human and has challenges at times.

"Language at times can get the best of me," he said. "In this game, things can happen that frustrate you, and you might say some words that aren't good, especially for a family to hear or see."

Now, he has his own son's opinion to consider.

"It's my goal," he added. "I know I have some little eyes and ears on me—and that will always be in the back of my mind."

Daniel's upbringing and his platform on the baseball field, combined with the addition to his family, make him want to be sure he uplifts the Lord more than anything else.

"I have a tremendous responsibility," he said. "I want everyone to know that I am a Christian, and that I'm not perfect, but I try each day to live my best for God."

> And he said to them, "Go into all the world and proclaim the gospel to the whole creation."
>
> —Mark 16:15

How do you let others know you are a child of God?

On Deck

Do you want those around you to know you are a follower of Christ? They probably are already aware of your favorite sports team or restaurant, but do they see your love and devotion for Christ? You might have some restrictions at work, or you may not want to offend anyone, but it is your obligation to the Creator to honor His name. But how?

Step Up to the Plate

You don't have to be in-your-face and obnoxious when it comes to sharing the love of the Lord. There are several subtle ways to let others know you are a Christian. In today's hypersensitive society, you also must be careful and use good judgment when it comes to sharing your faith. Here are some clever ways to get the point across in a way those around you will notice.

1. Social media. This is an effective way to communicate with your friends and followers. Make the effort to post things that are encouraging and uplifting to others and use scripture to reinforce your message. Mix it up and post other things of interest, but make sure you pepper in spiritual posts too. People love to be inspired and encouraged. Schedule a post each week with scripture. You can also post your favorite verse on your profile or include a statement that shows others that you love God.

2. Text messages. This is a good way to check up on your friends and let them know you are thinking about them and praying for them. Send positive text messages and words of encouragement. Make sure that nothing in your message is hurtful or can

be taken out of context, and remember that once you hit send, you can never get it back.

3. Cards. Holiday cards with scripture are a fantastic way to send the love of the Lord to your family and friends. Write personal notes in them to make them feel special.

4. Pray over your meals in public. This is a subtle way to show honor to God in front of others, and you may be surprised how many will respect you for doing this. Besides, God always deserves your thanks for His blessings in your life.

5. Email signature. When people receive your email, they will notice your signature. You can put something like "Blessed," "God loves you," or "Prayers" after your name.

6. Business cards. In addition to your contact information, include something that will point others to the fact that you are a believer. This might be one word, a statement, or even some artwork.

7. Decorations. Visit your local Christian Bible store or look online for home and office decor that will immediately provide a testimony to your guests about your love for God. It might help to open a door of opportunity for you to witness to others or connect with fellow believers.

8. Bible at work. Think about keeping a small Bible on your desk or inside your locker that people can see. Just like the decorations, this sends a message that you are a Christian and it might open the door for discussion with others.

9. Your car. You can use a license plate holder that has a Christian message or symbol that people see when they get behind you in traffic. Doing this adds responsibility to you as a driver, and you should obey traffic laws and treat other drivers with courtesy and professionalism.

10. Jewelry. Wear a necklace, bracelet, or watchband that has a cross or other icon on it that symbolizes your beliefs. More people will notice than you think, and it again may open doors for interesting conversations with others.

These are ideas you can use to let those around you know you are a Christian. You might have other ways, and that's great. Daniel uses his baseball glove and Twitter page to make everyone aware of his stance and allegiance to the Lord. But when you do this, be aware that many eyes will be on you and that you must be an ambassador for His army. Live your witness with a life of integrity and respect toward others and let everyone know that you are proud to serve God.

DAY 23

WHAT'S YOUR GO-TO VERSE?

David Hess:
Pitcher, Baltimore Orioles

By Del Duduit

I have been crucified with Christ. It is no longer I who live, but Christ who lives in me. And the life I now live in the flesh I live by faith in the Son of God, who loved me and gave himself for me.

—Galatians 2:20

Chances are if you ask a person what his or her favorite movie is, you will receive a quick reply.

The same goes if you inquire about a friend's favorite vacation spot or maybe a favorite meal.

But, how many people could tell you what their most treasured verse in the Bible might be? Could they recite it without looking?

David Hess can.

He's a pitcher for the Baltimore Orioles, but he can whip off Galatians 2:20 without blinking.

"It's one of my favorite verses because the verse, especially Paul, talks about his identity in Christ and who he is through what happened through Jesus' death and the resurrection," he said. "It just stands out as something that I want the world to be aware of and who I live for and who I play this game for."

This scripture has special meaning to David. He has others, too, but this one is his go-to verse.

"More than anything, it reminds me to be that example and representation Paul talks about," he said. "To be that representative every day."

David grew up in church in Tennessee. He learned values in Sunday school and made the decision on his own to follow Christ.

His faith developed while he attended and played baseball for Tullahoma High School. He later enrolled at Tennessee Technological University, where his performance led to him being drafted by Baltimore

But while he was in college, his faith became stronger, and his personal relationship with the Lord blossomed.

"Every day is a challenge; not just as an athlete but as a person in general," he said. "We come out here and play ball, and it's a challenge for our worth to be found in Christ alone and not in what the world says we should be or who we are."

This is why David relies on verses in the Word of God.

"I read it every day for strength and to draw closer to the Lord," he said. "But I have my go-to verses."

Delight yourself in the Lord,
and he will give you the desires of your heart.

—Psalm 37:4

Do you have a go-to verse you depend on to remind you what God has done for you? Can you recite it out loud right now?

On Deck

David has a reason behind the choice of his favorite verse. It means something to him. Perhaps you have gone through a personal struggle and you need words of encouragement to help you through difficult times. Many times, we choose a favorite scripture because it was one that God placed before us during a storm in our life, and it got our attention and helped us to remember how much God loves us. What is the story behind your life verse?

Step Up to the Plate

Everyone needs motivation and looks for something to give them a boost at just the right time. You are no different. If you haven't found your favorite verse yet, don't put too much thought into the process but instead let God reveal it to you when the time is right. You might stumble onto it during your daily devotions, and you may feel like you've been hit by a lightning bolt. You will know it when you see it. But in the meantime, here are some wonderful scriptures that many people fall back on and use as their go-to verses.

1. "Trust in the Lord with all your heart, / and do not lean on your own understanding" (Proverbs 3:5). We must believe in God who knows the whole picture when we can see only a piece of the puzzle. He knows what we need rather than what we think we might want or deserve.

2. "Call to me and I will answer you, and will tell you great and hidden things that you have not known" (Jeremiah 33:3). God has divine knowledge of all things, and He can show you the answers to your problems through His Word.

3. "I have stored up your word in my heart, / that I might not sin against you" (Psalm 119:11). When you are tempted to sin, bring your favorite verse to memory and say it out loud. Whisper the name of Jesus and ask for His divine protection.

4. "A good name is to be chosen rather than great riches, / and favor is better than silver or gold" (Proverbs 22:1). Don't choose a short-term desire over a long-term relationship with Jesus Christ. You can crumble in minutes what has taken you a lifetime to build. Seek God's wisdom through His Word and ask for leading from the Holy Spirit.

5. "But seek first the kingdom of God and his righteousness, and all these things will be added to you" (Matthew 6:33). Seek wise and godly counsel when an important decision must be made. Read the Word and pray for His plan, not yours.

6. "Jesus said to him, 'I am the way, and the truth, and the life. No one comes to the Father except through me'" (John 14:6). This is a great verse to use when you witness to others. The world can try to find peace a million different ways, but they can only get it through the shed blood of Jesus Christ on Calvary and remission of sins.

7. "I can do all things through him who strengthens me" (Philippians 4:13). We are helpless on our own, and we can only defeat Satan through the power of Christ. When you have worry or fear, say your favorite scripture and pray for God to lift you up and fill you with the Holy Spirit.

8. "For the wages of sin is death, but the free gift of God is eternal life in Christ Jesus our Lord" (Romans 6:23). It's difficult to understand why anyone would choose hell and the grave over heaven and eternal life. This verse is part of the Roman Road and is also great to use as you witness to others about their need for salvation.

9. "For God so loved the world, that he gave his only Son, that whoever believes in him should not perish but have eternal life" (John 3:16). God loved us so much that He temporarily gave up His most prized possession so that we would have a pathway to redemption. We can never thank Him enough for the sacrifice that He made for us so that we could live.

This is a suggested lineup for verses to commit to memory. Everyone is different and you must identify with a verse for it to become your own. Find one that is special to you.

By the way, David's favorite movie is *Gladiator*. His favorite vacation spot is anywhere that has a beach or mountains. And his favorite breakfast is bacon and eggs. "I'm a simple guy," he added. "That's what I like."

DAY 24
WHAT IS YOUR GIFT?

Al Oliver:
Batting Champion,
World Series Champion,
Pittsburgh Pirates

By Del Duduit

As each has received a gift, use it to serve one another, as good stewards of God's varied grace.

—1 Peter 4:10

From his early days at Portsmouth High School, Al Oliver knew he had talent when it came to baseball.

While he had great athletic skills, it was Al's responsibility to practice and become a top prospect.

All the years of dedication and hard work paid off over the years in Major League Baseball.

When his star-studded career ended, Al had posted a lifetime batting average of .303. He pounded out 2,743 hits and blasted 219 home runs.

In his seventeen years as a professional baseball player, he produced 1,326 RBIs.

"The Lord blessed me with athletic ability, especially as a hitter at the plate," Al said. "It just all came natural to me because God gave me that talent."

And when the pressure was on to produce at the plate, Al always came through.

When Al stepped into the batter's box with runners in scoring position, his average climbed to .320.

"I knew I could hit well with runners on base," he said. "I liked the feeling of pressure, and I knew I had to come through and I liked it."

In 1982, Al was the National League leader in RBIs and captured the Batting Title the same year.

Al thrived under pressure against some of the game's best pitchers. He enjoyed facing Bob Gibson and Jim Palmer, but he admitted he had issues when he batted against Steve Carlton.

"He was consistent and made me hit his best pitches— the pitches that were meant to get hitters out," Al said. "Even if I did make contact against Steve, it always seemed like it went right at his defensive players."

When Al faced Carlton, his average dropped to .197.

"He just had my number, and he was always tough to face," he said. "But I knew I had to try and keep swinging."

Having gifts that differ according to the grace given to us, let us use them: if prophecy, in proportion to our faith.
—Romans 12:6

On Deck

What special gift has God blessed you with? Some people recognize their calling early in the Christian walk while some, like me, don't find it until midlife or later. And there are times when you might not even realize what God wants you to do because you are in the way. You might want to sing, but you don't have the talent or a signal from the Lord to do that. There might be times when there is something specific you want to do for the Master, but He has not opened the doors. It can be a discouraging time when you have not been given the direction you long for. What do you do?

Step Up to the Plate

The best thing to do, but the last advice you want to hear, is to be patient. If you have not discovered what talent the Lord wants you to use, wait for Him and His guidance. But there are many "gifts" from God. As you journey with the Lord and seek His will, be mindful of what you believe He wants you to do for His glory. Here are some gifts to consider while you wait.

1. The gift of prayer. If you have ever been around a person with this gift, you know it right away. My friend Beckie, who wrote the chapter about Francisco Lindor, has this gift. We all talk and pray to the Lord, but some appear to have a unique way to commune with Him. Ask the Lord for this gift. "If you abide in me, and my words abide in you, ask whatever you wish, and it will be done for you" (John 15:7).

2. The gift of witnessing. For many, this is not easy. To talk to strangers about God's grace can cause many to become uncomfortable. But it needs to be done. Has God chosen you to do this? "For I

am not ashamed of the gospel, for it is the power of God for salvation to everyone who believes, to the Jew first and also to the Greek" (Romans 1:16).

3. The gift of charity. This is an area more need to become involved with. But there are a few who are called and have a gift to give. Ask for it if you want this gift.

4. The gift of singing. If you possess the gift of song or you can play a musical instrument, use your talents for the glory of God. Be sure to remain humble and make sure you do it to win souls to the Kingdom and to be a blessing to others, not for any applause or recognition. "Sing to God, sing praises to his name; / lift up a song to him who rides through the deserts; / his name is the Lord; / exult before him!" (Psalm 68:4).

5. The gift of writing. If you have a love and talent to begin a writing ministry, then ask the Lord to open doors for you. I did that when I was fifty years old. But be ready, because when He answered my prayers, my life became very busy and was changed forever. I'm so thankful to Him for his many blessings since this journey began.

6. The gift of praise. Notice I did not say the gift of discouragement or telling everyone your problems. The gift of praise is one we all need to have. Strive to lift up the name of the Lord in all you do. "Praise the Lord! / Oh give thanks to the Lord, for he is good, / for his steadfast love endures forever!" (Psalm 106:1).

7. The gift of encouragement. This gift is one that
    I wish more people were blessed with. It seems
    like so many tear down their fellow man. We need
    more people who will send out a text or an email or
    make a phone call to inspire others. A few positive
    words and some well-timed scripture can change
    the whole outlook for a person in need.

Al knew early what his earthly talents were going to be. He
had no doubt. After he finished his MLB career, he became
a deacon in his church. He is also an inspirational speaker.
He knows his calling and is thankful for his gift. Ask the
Lord what He wants you to do. Be patient and, when you
receive the go-ahead signal, use your talents and gifts to
praise and honor the Lord.

DAY 25
MAKE AN ENTRANCE

Corey Dickerson:
All-Star Outfielder,
Philadelphia Phillies

By Del Duduit

Go ye therefore, and teach all nations, baptizing them in the name of the Father, and of the Son, and of the Holy Ghost.

—Matthew 28:19 KJV

The walk-out song is big in the MLB.

Many of the players put a lot of thought and consideration into the music that is played when they are introduced as they approach home plate and get ready to hit the ball.

Some of them select the same song or tune for the year, while others change it up each week.

The song that is played when they make their stroll from the on-deck circle to the batter's box says a lot about their personality.

During the 2018 season, Corey Dickerson chose to play the music of contemporary Christian artist Jeremy Camp each time he was at bat. He identifies with the music and says he wants to send a message to the fans that he is a follower of Jesus Christ.

"I like to pick my music because of the kids who come to the games," he said. "With the large platform we have as players, I try to put a lot of thought into it, and I want to make sure it's appropriate and sends a positive message."

Corey said since he's not able to interact with the fans as much as he would like, the songs and walk-out music can provide a glimpse into who he is as a person.

"It's important to avoid drama, stay out of trouble, and be positive," he said. "That's why I like to let everyone know I am a Christian, and this is just one way."

For about two years, Corey chose Camp's song, "Take My Life," as his introduction when he came to the plate.

A portion of the song talks about surrendering your life to the Lord. "It's just a powerful song," Corey said. "One that hits home with me."

With young children at home, Corey said he wants to be a positive role model as a father and influence his kids to follow the Lord.

"The toughest part of this job is being gone a lot," he said. "But as they get older and I see how much they change, I want to be there and be a part of it. But at the same time, this game is short, so I need to make the most of it now."

His image is important to him, and he also values the time he gets to spend with his family when he is off the road.

"When my kids hear my name in the news or anything like that, I want it to be good," Corey said. "That is huge to me. I want them to think of me as a good player but also as a good person and dad."

> Study to shew thyself approved unto God, a workman that needeth not to be ashamed, rightly dividing the word of truth.
>
> —2 Timothy 2:15 KJV

If you could pick a song to be played when you walk into work each day, what would it be?

On Deck

Perhaps you have moved into a different neighborhood or started a new job. You want to make a good first impression and let everyone know you are a follower of the Lord. At the same time, you want to be accepted and not labeled in a negative way. But you know your responsibility is to your own identify and to your Lord. Find a way to let everyone around know you love Christ.

Step Up to the Plate

If you could select a song that could describe your life, there are many to choose from. Some are fast with a good beat while others are slow and dramatic. Everyone has a story. Here are some selections to consider for your life song.

1. "All the People Said Amen" by Matt Maher. There is power in the word *amen*. It signifies agreement among your brothers and sisters in Christ. You have to establish unity in your spirit with others in order to do the will of God. When you are unified with others, you can knock the devil down with

a fastball high and tight. Be a strong part of your community and let everyone know whose team you are on.

2. "Do Something" by Matthew West. You cannot sit by and watch sin ruin the lives of people around you. Do something. Spread the gospel of the Lord in your own way, whether it be through social media, witnessing, or inviting your friends to church.

3. "Write Your Story" by Francesca Battistelli. You have a unique story because it's your own. You were changed and left a life of sin to begin a journey that includes peace and eternal life with Christ. Some people are ashamed of their past and fear judgment from others. But your story can give you the ability to reach people who might have experienced the same pain you did. Tell them how God changed your life.

The message you portray has an impact. You might be able to influence a few people or hundreds each day. Don't take the responsibility to share God's love for granted. Walk out to a wonderful song of praise.

DAY 26

BE PASSIONATE IN YOUR SERVICE

Tim Tebow:
Outfielder,
New York Mets

By Del Duduit

So, whether you eat or drink, or whatever you do, do all to the glory of God.

—1 Corinthians 10:31

When Tim was a young child, he signed up for youth baseball at Normandy Baseball Park. He was put on the White Sox and picked number 35, the same number worn by slugger Frank Thomas.

Even at such a young age, he was passionate about baseball.

"I loved it, and I picked number 35 because I wanted to be Frank Thomas," he said. "Most of my life, I thought I was going to be a professional baseball player."

But his talent in football came to national prominence when he was a junior in high school. His competitiveness and running ability caught the attention of college scouts. But one night after he played an entire second half with a broken fibula, he was finished for the season.

Even with the injury, he was named Florida's High School Player of the Year.

The next year, he guided the Nease Panthers to a state title, earned All-State honors, and was named Florida's Mr. Football. He also captured the Player of the Year award for the second time.

But still, he wanted to play on the diamond instead of the gridiron.

The University of Florida Head Coach Urban Meyer recruited Tim to play football, which was encouraged by his mother.

"When your mom wants you to get an education, and then Urban recruits you, it was hard to pass, let's just say that," Tim said with a laugh. "We talked about it, and I wanted to play, but I also wanted to play on the baseball team too."

Tim's accomplishments as a Gator are remarkable:

- Two BCS National Championships
- Two Southeast Conference Championships
- Two Southeast Conference Player of the Year Awards
- Two Maxwell Awards
- AP Player of the Year
- Sporting News Player of the Year
- Three First Team All-SEC selections
- Manning Award
- Heisman Trophy

Obviously, Tim had a talent for playing college football.

He was drafted by the Denver Broncos and played two seasons before going to the New York Jets for one.

Although he made it to the big show, he still wanted to play baseball.

"I want to live a life I am passionate about, and when I told a few guys who were my agents I wanted to play baseball, it was just crickets," he said. "Then Brody walked into the room, and he said he would watch me play. We flew to Boca Raton, and after that he became my agent and put me in position to play baseball."

In 2016, Tim signed on with the New York Mets organization.

He has played at all levels in the minor league system, and he knew making it to the big leagues was not going to be easy.

"I'm enjoying myself right now and loving it," he said. "I try to enjoy each day regardless of how it goes. I'm living a dream every single day."

There have been days when he has not played well or the media has written negative things about his performance. Still, he knows that is not what matters.

"There are always ups and downs in this game and in life," he said. "But it's how you handle it, and it's about perspective. Regardless of what others say about you, don't ever let them define you. Only one person gets to define you, and that's the God of this universe. Go live your dream."

I can do all things through him who strengthens me.
—Philippians 4:13

How is your passion to serve the Lord and others? Who or what defines you?

On Deck

Have you ever had a dream but other opportunities came first? Maybe you have a passion to be a writer but had to do other jobs to make ends meet. Perhaps you always wanted to be a pastor, but you needed to hold down a job for financial reasons. Or maybe you have a passion to go to the mission field, but you decided to enter the corporate world and plan for retirement.

Step Up to the Plate

Granted, there is only one Tim Tebow. He has been blessed with ability and has earned a good living. He could have easily taken other roads toward success, but he was passionate about playing baseball. He chased his dream, turned a deaf ear to the critics, and listened to his advocates. Maybe like Tim, you have a passion to do something other than what you are currently doing. But can you fulfill your dreams?

1. Tell God what you want. Be specific and thank Him for all the opportunities He has given you. Nothing is too big or too small for the Lord to provide. "In that day you will ask nothing of me. Truly, truly, I say unto you, whatever you ask of the Father in my name, he will give it to you" (John 16:23).
2. Dive deeper into the Word. Increase the time you spend reading the Bible and make it a point to do this each day. Study the scripture diligently and ask Him to reveal what He has for you each day.

3. Increase your prayer time and fast. Refrain from food or from something that distracts your time with God, such as social media or watching television. Then devote that extra time to spend with the Lord and to commune with Him. Make this time special and pour out your heart to Him. "Pray without ceasing" (1 Thessalonians 5:17).

4. Avoid negative people. There are people in your life who never encourage you to succeed and always focus on the negative. Embrace those who will cheer you on and encourage you to meet your goals. If it's your own family being negative, pray for God to change their hearts.

5. Ask God to open doors. Ask the Lord to prepare you and to provide a way to make your dream a reality. Be specific and then be patient. Don't get in the way and try to make things happen yourself. Wait on the Lord, and be ready when he calls your name to get into the game. "Now faith is the assurance of things hoped for, the conviction of things not seen" (Hebrews 11:1).

Many of Tim's colleagues did not believe he could play professional baseball except for one. Tim stuck by that person and trusted him to help him get to the next level. Tim also put his trust in God and went through the doors that opened for him. No matter what you dream of doing, know that if you seek and trust God, He will lead you down the right path. Be passionate about the Lord first and His will for your life, and the rest will fall into place.

DAY 27
YOU ARE SPECIAL TO GOD

Clint Hurdle:
MLB Player and Coach,
Retired

By Del Duduit

> But God commendeth his love toward us, in that, while we
> were yet sinners, Christ died for us.
>
> —Romans 5:8 KJV

Clint Hurdle is my friend.

I was happy for him when he decided to hang up his
pants and retire after a long and productive career in the
MLB.

During his tenure as a player and a coach, he saw the ups
and downs.

He was traded as a player and fired as a manager. But
overall, he loved his career in the big leagues, especially
when he guided the Colorado Rockies to the World Series
in 2007.

In 2011, he took over at Pittsburgh and helped to turn
the franchise around.

He is loved in the steel city for his fiery defense of his
players, and for his devotion to his family.

Clint has a daughter through a previous marriage and two
children with his current wife, Karla. They have a daughter

who was born with Prader-Willi Syndrome. People who have this genetic disorder don't know when they are full.

"They feel hungry their entire life," Clint said. "From the time they wake up until they go to bed, they are hungry."

This is because chromosome 15, the one that regulates hunger, is missing.

As a result, some who suffer from this syndrome have delayed growth and motor skills.

"My daughter didn't walk until she was twenty months old and didn't run until she was four," he said. "We had to get our heads around this early."

She needed complete structure in her life, and Clint and Karla prayed for guidance.

"We all have challenges," he said. "I'm a recovering alcoholic, and we all have needs. God is omnipresent, and in His wisdom, He gave her to us to take care of."

Through it all, Clint's relationship with his wife grew stronger. They had to play as a team for their daughter's sake.

"That's the unconditional love you have for each other, and we have that," he said. "You stand in the gap for one another."

There are many things that can lead to the breakup of the family such as financial troubles or job relocations. But taking care of a child with special needs is a huge hurdle for a married couple to face. But in this case, it brought them closer together.

Clint and Karla have taken care of their daughter as a team, and she is doing well with her condition. They help her with her diet and exercise as well as schoolwork, and

DUGOUT DEVOTIONS II

they take her to therapy. It can be a challenge at times, but they have adjusted.

"I have special needs, you have special needs," Clint said. "Hers is in a different context."

> I will praise thee, for I am fearfully and wonderfully made: marvellous are thy works; and that my soul knoweth right well.
>
> —Psalm 139:14 KJV

On Deck

Clint was right when he said that everyone has special needs. His has been his battle with alcohol that he has overcome with the help of the Lord and good friends. His support system is in place. But you might have a special need no one knows about. How will you obtain the help you need to overcome it? You might have a physical condition or a financial problem that needs to be addressed. Or perhaps you stand in need of something greater such as salvation. Perhaps you need healing or restoration of your marriage.

Step Up to the Plate

No matter what you face, the first thing you need to do is to make sure the Lord is batting in the leadoff position in your lineup. Clint and his family put Christ first, and they know He will meet every need they have. Whether it's getting up early to help their daughter catch the bus or coming home early to do the laundry so the other can take a nap, teamwork is the best solution. It's important to have a strong support system. But what if you don't? That's when you need to lean on God and let Him show you the way. You are special in His eyes and He will help you through any situation you have. Ask Him to put godly and wise people on your team. Here are some ways Jesus makes you feel special.

1. He forgives you. This is huge, but He will only do this if you ask him to. Your sins must be forgiven in order for you to make it into the kingdom of God. Believe in his mercies and make a promise to serve Him today. "For thou, Lord, art good, and ready to forgive; and plenteous in mercy unto all them that call upon thee" (Psalm 86:5 KJV).

2. He provides and take care of you. The Lord will give you what need to make it through each day if you have faith believing that He will. Notice I did not say what you *want*. You might not have the biggest house on the block or drive a new car, but He will give you the essentials. Look to Him for the answers to all of your prayers and always give Him the glory. "Trust in him at all times; ye people, pour out your heart before him: God is a refuge for us. Selah" (Psalm 62:8 KJV).

3. He loves you. If you have children, would you send one of them to die for someone else's sin? I would never agree to do that. The Lord did just that because He loves you. "For God so loved the world, that he gave his only begotten Son, that

whosoever believeth in him should not perish, but have everlasting life" (John 3:16 KJV).

4. He will not forsake you. When times are bleak and friends are hard to find, the Lord will always be there to comfort you. Friends may come and go, but the Master will always show up when the game is on the line. "And the Lord, he it is that doth go before thee; he will be with thee, he will not fail thee, neither forsake thee: fear not, neither be dismayed" (Deuteronomy 31:8 KJV).

5. He has prepared a place for you. Rest assured, once you make the decision to follow Christ, you are guaranteed a spot on his team in heaven, if you don't opt out of your contract. Stay on the squad and do your best to live for Him. "And if I go and prepare a place for you, I will come again, and receive you unto myself; that where I am, there ye may be also" (John 14:3 KJV).

Clint said it best when he described us all as having special needs. In God's eyes, you are special. That's why He forgives you, provides for you, loves you, protects you, and has prepared a place for you. All you have to do is accept His gift.

DAY 28
START THE CONVERSATION

Curtis Granderson:
All-Star Outfielder,
Miami Marlins

By Del Duduit

He put a new song in my mouth,
a song of praise to our God.
Many will see and fear,
and put their trust in the Lord.

—Psalm 40:3

Have you ever had that awkward moment when you don't know what to say or how to say it?

Maybe you want to share your faith, and it just doesn't seem right. The last thing you want to do is force the issue and come off in the wrong fashion.

Everyone has these moments, even professional baseball players.

Curtis Granderson, who was chosen as one of the friendliest players in the MLB from a poll of 290 players by *Sports Illustrated*, also knows not to shove his faith down the throat of a nonbeliever.

"Talking with people happens organically," he said. "A lot of people assume in general that as soon as someone comes into the locker room, that we know them. That's not the case. You have to make the effort to talk with them, about everything, including their faith and the game and life in general."

Throughout the course of any day, you may have a lot of activities going on. Your boss might want to talk with you or your spouse may ask you to run an errand. You need to focus on your work, and so does Curtis. He is paid to be good at his craft of playing baseball, and that takes of lot of time and effort.

"Sometimes a discussion about my faith might come up, and it might not," he said. "You have to know the circumstances and have a feel for the moment too."

For example, Curtis told me in 2019, he had been to chapel a few times with a player on the team, but he hadn't spoken to him about his faith yet.

"It's not that we choose not to, it just hadn't come up yet. We hadn't had the chance to talk one-on-one," he said. "Will we? Most likely. We spend a lot of time together as teammates, and I know we will get around to talking to each other soon enough."

Once the topic is introduced, it makes the conversations easier.

"Most of our conversations I've had with other players came about and started with something else," he added. "Like where did you go to college? Where did you grow up? That can lead to discussions about faith. I like to pepper into conversations about my faith, like where I went to church, you know, stuff like that. But the initial conversation wasn't about God, but it can lead that way."

Curtis takes opportunities to share his faith when it does become appropriate. He knows the topic won't present itself during batting practice, but then again it might.

"You just have to know the circumstance and decipher the right moments," he said. "But the bottom line is when it does come up, you need to be ready and tell about how good God has been."

The point here is you never know when a conversation about the Lord might take place.

> Do your best to present yourself to God as one approved, a worker who has no need to be ashamed, rightly handling the word of truth.
>
> —2 Timothy 2:15

Are you ready for the talk? Will you share your testimony of faith to your coworkers or colleagues?

On Deck

Maybe you are on a company retreat and have some casual time with people you know but may not know well. What will the conversation sound like? Will you talk sports, politics, the weather, or careers? Those are all appropriate topics, but will you eventually get around to your faith?

Step Up to the Plate

You should not be confrontational or judgmental when you discuss your testimony. You want to make sure everyone knows about your faith, but you also want to present it at the right time. There are easy ways to work it into a conversation. You can throw in examples like, "I had a similar conversation with a friend of mine at church Sunday" or "several of the guys at church watched the game, too, and had the same reaction." There are many ways to lead the dialogue toward speaking about the Lord. But before you do, check out these tips that might help you when you share your faith.

1. Don't assume. You might know that the person you are going to speak with doesn't go to church, but you don't know their story. Maybe they had a bad experience while attending church in the past, or maybe they are upset with God about a tragedy in their family. Listen and show understanding, and then let them know how much your church family means to you.

2. Be interested. Pay attention to what people say and how they feel. If they see that you have a genuine interest in them, they may feel more comfortable and might consider opening up to you.

3. Know what you are talking about. This comes through practice. Curtis spends hours hitting and fielding balls to be ready for each game. You must spend time in prayer and reading the Word of God. Commit some verses to memory that tell of God's goodness. Be ready to explain why God loves them, and how they can come to Christ for forgiveness. Practice.

4. Share your experience. Be honest and relate to the person you talk with. Don't start a contest for worst sinner, but be honest about your past mistakes and let them know how God forgave you and gave you grace, mercy, and peace. Show them how you can relate to their past and how you found the best way to deal with life's struggles. "Your word is a lamp to my feet / and light to my path" (Psalm 119:105).

5. Let them decide. The last thing you want to do is become a bully. Once you share your faith with them, ask them if they want to experience the same God you serve. If they do, then that's great and you can show them how to become a Christian. If they refuse, then you have done your part and planted the seed, and you can tell them to let you know if or when they're ready to join the family of God.

You want to do your part as a member of the Lord's team. Make sure you are always ready to lay down the bunt when the Coach gives you the signal.

DAY 29
THE AHA MOMENT

**Spencer Turnbull:
Pitcher,
Detroit Tigers**

By Del Duduit

Anyone who does not love does not know God, because
God is love.

—1 John 4:8

Spencer Turnbull likes to post inspirational messages on
Twitter. He makes it clear that he loves the Lord on his
profile page where he states that he is a "Believer in Jesus
Christ" and lists Ephesians 3:19–20.

"It's just part of who I am," he said. "It's what I believe,
and I like to post stuff like that because that has helped
me."

He feels like it's his responsibility to share the love of
Christ with others. "It's my platform, and it's what I'm
called to do and use it for."

Spencer tries to use his social media in a positive way,
but he admits that not everyone likes or agrees with his
posts. But he's okay with that.

He grew up in church in a Southern Bible Belt culture.
Spencer was involved in the youth group and attended
vacation Bible school. This was his way of life.

"I really enjoyed that lifestyle because it was fun, and it was all I knew," he added. "But it was something I did because all my friends did it—it wasn't really something I was sure I believed in, personally."

But toward the end of his senior year in high school, he had a life-changing experience after he walked through a Barnes & Noble bookstore one day and passed a book that grabbed his attention.

It was *Mere Christianity* by C. S. Lewis.

He started to read it, then took it home and couldn't put it down.

Four chapters into the book, he had his "aha" moment.

"[The author] answered a lot of questions I had about Christianity," Spencer said. "Things that were always in the back of my mind. That was when I realized that Jesus is real. Before that, I wasn't sure and wanted to think He was real. But I always had some doubts. After that book, there was no more doubt. Jesus was real from that moment on."

This was a big relief for Spencer, who truly knows Christ is the answer for any problem.

"We all have daily challenges and struggles; that's life," he said. "It might be security, thoughts, or unbelief—but God is there."

He said the consistent battles of the flesh that the devil throws at professional athletes is the biggest challenge. "It's easy to get tired spiritually, and it can be hard to stay ready for the fights. That's been my biggest struggle—for me—being consistent."

When he's home with friends, family, and his church, life is much easier. "It's not as tough when you're around your support system. But I have to lean on God more when I'm away. But knowing what I know now makes it easier."

> You will seek me and find me, when you seek me with all your heart.
>
> —Jeremiah 29:13

Do you remember your "aha" moment when God became real in your life? Have you had that experience?

On Deck

Maybe you are like Spencer and grew up in church and that's all you knew. You enjoyed your friends at youth group and the church was a big part of your life. But do you remember that moment when you decided to follow Christ? If you can't remember, then you might want to reexamine your commitment to the Lord. You don't want to go through the motions and discover you are not a Christian when it's too late. You are the one person responsible for your own salvation. You are the only one who can ask God into your heart.

Step Up to the Plate

Maybe you are a Christian and have a good life but might find yourself in a rut. You need your own "aha" moment to take you to the next level in your walk with Christ. Here are some "aha" moments that can help you along the way.

1. You don't have to please everyone. You cannot control what others think about you. The only thing you can do is to be honest and friendly. If someone you work with or go to church with doesn't like you, and you have made a genuine effort to get along with them to no avail, then toss it to the side like a foul ball. Give the situation to God, and do your best to always please Him. Aha!

2. Do your best to live a transparent life. Everyone has their own calling in life. Spencer is a professional ball player but makes sure those who see his Twitter feed know he is a Christian. He is open about his faith and his struggles. This will only make him stronger and more accountable. The same goes for you. Let those around you know who you serve and know that you are not perfect but that you trust in a God who is flawless. Aha!

3. Stay within your means. Some people are blessed with financial security while others struggle to make ends meet. Don't go into debt to keep up with the neighbors or to impress others. This can put chains on your spiritual freedom by enslaving you to others. Be who you are and live accordingly. Aha!

4. Choices have consequences. Every decision you make will have a result. Impulse buys or spur-of-the-moment decisions can come back to bite you, and you cannot hide from God. He sees and knows what you are doing. Some people might be temporarily fooled by the choices you make, but

someday God will bring your sin into the light. Make good decisions. Aha!

5. No excuses. Take responsibility for your actions and decisions. You seek the recognition when good things happen, so accept responsibility when negative things happen. Don't make an excuse for why you don't attend church. Don't make an excuse for not reading your Bible. Make these priorities in your life. Aha!

Spencer experienced his moment in a Barnes & Noble bookstore. God is everywhere and will reveal Himself when you least expect it to happen. If the Lord answers your prayer—Aha! If God calls you to do something great for His glory—Aha! Be open to the possibility that He will show up on time, every time. Be ready and accept your moment.

DAY 30
GROW WITH THE WORD

Jacob Stallings:
Catcher,
Pittsburgh Pirates

By Del Duduit

But grow in grace and knowledge of our Lord and Savior
Jesus Christ. To him be the glory both now and to the day
of eternity. Amen.

—2 Peter 3:18

Jacob Stallings grew up in church in Kansas. He attended a
Christian high school and enjoyed a good life.

During his senior year of high school, his faith started to
blossom. He started to ask a lot of questions when he was a
freshman in college.

He wanted to do more for the Lord and wanted to spread
his wings and grow in his faith.

Jacob started to search for churches that offered what he
lacked.

"I just needed to grow," he said. "I knew there was
something for me, and I had to go find it."

He began to attend a nondenominational church and
enjoyed the atmosphere and spirit.

The same year, he had several conversations with his
girlfriend (now his wife), who was a big support to him.

"She is amazing in her faith, and I don't know what I'd do without her," he said. "She's been my rock."

Both were going through the same struggles of being homesick and wanted to do more for God and grow spiritually.

One day, Jacob heard one of his college teammates, who is now a pastor, talk about the historical facts of Jesus and His life here on earth.

"There is no arguing that He was here on this planet," he said. "But for some, the argument might be about who He was. Just listening to the conversation, because I love history, I started to dive deeper into the Word of God."

His friend gave him the book, *More Than a Carpenter* by Josh McDowell. "It's by far my favorite, next to the Bible, of course," he said.

The more Jacob read, the more he felt something begin to move.

"I kept reading the Bible, reading the book, and I felt myself getting stronger," he said. "I knew I was growing."

Jacob surrounds himself with people who are like-minded. And that helps when he's on the road playing baseball.

"The challenges are being away from my family, and that's hard," he said. "The lifestyles of some of the guys in the league are a little different than mine, and that's a challenge at times too."

When Jacob discovered the Scriptures and really made an effort to study the Word of God more, he started to grow in his faith.

"The more you can surround yourself with believers and with people of faith, the better you'll be, and you'll be able to talk about some of your troubles," he said. "But it all goes back to wanting to grow and become stronger."

For we walk by faith, not by sight.

—2 Corinthians 5:7

Can you find a way to grow? Are you satisfied with where you are on your Christian journey, or is there room for improvement?

On Deck

You have heard the saying that if you are not moving forward, then you are moving backward. The same applies to your walk of faith. Where are you right now? Are you involved in activities that will help strengthen your Christian beliefs? Do you spend time in the Word of God each day to become stronger? How is your prayer life? Are there areas where you could improve on it to put you on a more solid foundation?

Step Up to the Plate

The answer to the last question for everyone should be yes. As a catcher, Jacob knows he must continue to work out and practice to see playing time. If he slacks off, he will get passed by those working harder. There are many ways to increase your faith and grow your spiritual life. Don't wait until you are in a weakened state to make some changes. A flower needs water and sunlight to blossom, and a follower of Jesus needs to read the Bible, pray, and fellowship with others. Here are some suggestions for ways to grow your faith each day.

1. Hear the Word. This can be accomplished by attending church on a regular basis. The Pittsburgh Pirates have no chance to win a game if they do not show up at the stadium. The same is true for you. You must hear what God says. Take your family to church and Sunday school every time you can. Don't settle for less and duck out of church and make excuses. There is something special about being there in person. Get up and go to the house of God. "So faith comes from hearing, and hearing through the word of Christ" (Romans 10:17).

2. Believe the Word. It's one thing to listen to the Word, and it's another to believe what it says and put it into action. Jacob grew up in a Christian environment but had to make his own decision to trust what he read. It's a wonderful day when you come to the point where you believe in the inspired Word of God. Try to make each day you read the Bible fresh and exciting. Don't go through the motions to please the Lord—He knows your heart, and you are better than that. Find a time to get away to yourself and read the Scriptures—then trust in what you read. The devil will fill your head with lies and send people into your life to confuse you. But at the end of the day, stand on the truth of the Word of God and believe in God's promises.

"But he said, 'blessed rather are those who hear the word of God and keep it!'" (Luke 11:28).

3. Act on the Word. The instructions to live a wonderful life are in the pages of the Bible. Read it. Study it. Act on it. Live by it. Pray and seek His will. This does not mean your life will be problem-free, but His Word will help, guide, and comfort you on your journey.

Jacob was mature enough in his faith to realize he wanted more from God. He wasn't content to go through the motions to please those around him. He discovered a deeper and richer faith once he made the decision to find what God had to offer. You can do the same.

Made in the USA
Las Vegas, NV
12 December 2022

62132317R00096